The Little Book

of

British History

The Little Book
of
British History

by

DUNCAN GUNN

First published in 1999 by Mustard
Mustard is an imprint of Parragon

Parragon
Queen Street House
4 Queen Street
Bath BA1 1HE UK

Produced by Magpie Books, an imprint of
Robinson Publishing Ltd, London

ISBN 1 84164 266 5

A copy of the British Library Cataloguing-in-Publication Data is
available from the British Library

Contents

❧

8: The Twentieth Century   223

The Playboy King – George V – World War I –
Independence for Ireland – Votes for Women! – The
General Strike – Love Conquers All – George VI –
World War II – Sir Winston Churchill – A Social
Revolution – Elizabeth II: A Truly Modern Monarch

Introduction

Britain has played a major role on the world stage for so long it is difficult to imagine what the modern world would look like if this little group of islands off the coast of Europe had not been united through many long centuries of war, bitter rivalry, uneasy compromise and occasional trickery.

There would not, for instance, be a United States of America. That great nation owes its birth in 1766 to the stubborn greed of a British government which refused to acknowledge the injustice of taxing people 3,000 miles away while offering them no say in how those taxes were spent.

Without the great academic institutions founded in Britain there would not have been the research facilities which resulted in the unraveling of the DNA molecule, the discovery of penicillin or the invention of radar and jet engines. And it is British inventors we have to thank for the steam engine, the mass-production of iron and steel, inflatable tires and the durable road surfaces on which those wheels roll.

It was only a matter of time before the rest of the world learned of the existence of lands such as Australia, New Zealand and many of the inhabited islands which dot the Earth's oceans. In many cases it was British explorers and adventurers who brought that news back and redrew the maps. And it was an Englishman, Sir Francis Drake, who first circumnavigated the globe in the 16th century.

Along the way, British artists, poets, playwrights, actors and musicians have created a volume of work which still stands as a beacon of beauty, grandeur and continued inspiration: Shakespeare, Dickens, Chaucer, Milton, Robert Burns, Dylan Thomas, Wordsworth, Keats, Shelley and Byron, for instance, along with the likes of Turner, Constable and Stubbs, jostle for space in the definitive collections of literature and art. And where would pop music be today without The Beatles, or a film world lacking Elizabeth Taylor, Cary Grant, Sean Connery, Anthony Hopkins and David Lean? Or modern art without David Hockney, Lucien Freud and Damien Hirst?

And let us not forget that it was Britain which gave

the rest of the world the games of cricket, rugby football, golf and association football. Not bad for a nation
which is only a third the size of Texas!

1

The Romans in Britain
AD 43–406

❖

The Romans occupied and ruled much of the British Isles for around 400 years from AD 43. They had visited England earlier, in 55 BC, when Julius Caesar shipped a force of 10,000 men from Gaul (now France) to the Kent coast. He was forced to retreat when storms cut him off from supplies and reinforcements. A year later Caesar returned with 25,000 infantry and 2,000 cavalry, forcing his Celtic opponents into surrender before departing.

Most of what we know about British society in this period comes from Roman records, for the Celts did not write their own history. Archaeology and science have since given a fuller picture. We now know that Britain's original inhabitants were hunter-gatherers who used stone implements to clear land for cultivation from around 4000 BC. By 2500 BC they were using bronze and copper tools to turn forests into farms.

Migrating European Celts brought iron tools and weapons and introduced the first enclosed fields to the British landscape, along with a crop rotation system. Formidable fighters and skilled artists, the Celts continually fought among each other for land and title. This internal disharmony made the Romans' task easier when they finally launched their all-out invasion of AD 43.

After defeating the forces of Caratacus the Romans pushed on to establish a base from which they could mount successful offensives on the enemy. Colchester became the first Roman city in Britain. Eleven British kings surrendered to the Emperor Claudius, leaving his army clear to begin conquering other parts of the country.

After subduing a revolt led by Boudicca, queen of the Iceni, the Romans seized the rest of southern England before taking most of Wales, founding a new fortress-city at Chester, defeating the northern Brigante tribe and building an army headquarters at York.

With most of Wales and England under Roman

rule, in AD 79 General Agricola invaded Scotland. The Romans would never succeed in holding the north, and in AD 122 the Emperor Hadrian conceded defeat by ordering the construction of a massive fortified wall between the mouth of the River Tyne in the east (near modern-day Newcastle) to Bowness, on the River Solway, to the west. This marked the northern-most boundary of the Roman Empire until the Emperor Antonine built the smaller wall 20 years later, which stretched from modern Edinburgh to east of Glasgow.

Under the Romans Britain adopted Roman law, religion, building styles, fashions and domestic life. Many of the country's natives were taken as slaves, and Celtic warriors were ordered home to tend their farms. New Roman towns were built, as were grand villas, complete with under-floor heating and bathing pools. Pottery, fabrics and precious metalware were imported from Europe, along with Italian and Greek traders. Inevitably and inexorably, British "wannabes" began building their own versions of Roman houses and began wearing the toga to mark their Romanization.

Romans built the first roads and developed large sea-ports. Trade and industry flourished, bringing wines from Italy, Germany and Spain, fish sauces and olive oil from Spain, as well as the concept of paying for goods and services with coins. Structured government was introduced, and the practice of gardening for aesthetic pleasure. While the Romans initially imposed their religion of many gods and goddesses, by AD 400 they were promoting Christianity, which had become Rome's state religion.

The Roman Empire began to fragment and crumble during the late 4th century. During the century before the Romans finally pulled their army out of Britain, they were subjected to a growing number of raids by Saxons – from what is now northern Germany and southern Denmark. Worn down by internal rebellions by British tribes, the final Roman exodus came in AD 406, leaving Britain to face the Saxons alone.

The Roman occupation of Britain was over.

The Celts

✤

𝔄 "family" of tribes who occupied most of Europe from the 4th century BC, the Celts originated in what is now central Europe and established themselves eastwards as far as Asia Minor and as far west as the British Isles long before either the Greek or Roman empires were founded.

It was the Celts who first worked iron, so creating the formidable weapons with which they overcame their early enemies. Their artistic heritage is rich in beautifully wrought gold and silverware, pottery and ceremonial armor, much of which has been found in the burial sites explored by archaeologists during the past 200 years.

So gifted were Celtic jewelers and armorers that the Romans employed Celts during their own expansion. And the ferocity of Celtic warriors became so renowned across the known world that the Egyptian queen, Cleopatra, employed Celts as her personal bodyguards, while some of the best Roman cavalry units were comprised almost exclusively of Celtic horsemen.

Founders of a tightly structured, complex and deeply religious society, the Celts also pioneered the science of rotation farming. And while the Romans may have introduced bath-houses to Britain, it was the Celts who introduced them to soap – something they'd invented some centuries earlier!

Boudicca

✦

Wife and queen of Prasatugas – the king of the Iceni tribe which dominated most of what is now East Anglia – Boudicca came to personify Celtic resistance in the early years of Roman occupation.

During his reign Prasatugas signed a peace treaty with the Romans. Boudicca intended to keep to the terms of that treaty when her husband died in AD 60, but when local Roman authorities seized his property with an attack in which Boudicca's two daughters were raped, she formed an alliance with the Trinovantes, whose lands had also been sequestered, and began a campaign of attrition.

Described by one Roman commentator as having "a harsh voice," Boudicca was also said to be "very tall," her appearance made all the more striking by "a great mass of red hair" that cascaded to her hips. Her army had successfully captured and burned Colchester, London and St Albans before the governor of Britain, Suetonius Paulinus, amassed the biggest force he could.

Paulinus cornered his enemy in the Midlands. In the battle that followed, more than 80,000 Celts were slaughtered. Boudicca evaded capture by killing herself with poison. The most startling proof of Boudicca's existence and achievements in war has been found by archaeologists in the deep layer of red, burned clay which lies under the streets of modern-day London — evidence that her forces did indeed destroy the city in a great all-consuming fire.

Death of the Druids

✤

Druids occupied a unique position in Celtic tribal hierarchy, being more or less equal in status to the nobility. There is ample evidence that their roles included those of bard (or storyteller), doctor, legal arbiter, musician and master craftsman. In a society whose religion, history and laws survived only through the spoken word, the Druid was a key player.

As the Romans began their sweep through Britain, it was inevitable that many tribal leaders would be killed and more compliant people appointed to act as puppet chieftains. It follows that Druids suffered the same fate, for Rome was determined to inflict its own laws and religious practices on all "savages" they encountered.

Matters came to a head in AD 60 when Suetonius Paulinus launched a last great offensive against Welsh rebels on the island of Anglesey. This had also become the principal refuge for a large number of surviving Druids and the place from which they continued to urge Britons to fight on.

In his own description of the battle, Paulinus recounted how the enemy massed on the shore: "Between the ranks dashed women in black, like the Furies, with their hair let down and streaming, and brandishing flaming torches." If that was not frightening enough, Paulinus noted that "around the enemy host were Druids, uttering prayers and curses."

It is possible that some Druids managed to escape the massacre which followed, but those survivors would prove no match for the inexorable rise of Roman rule in England and Wales and the imposition of Roman gods and festivals on a vanquished population.

Druids would continue to play their part in Ireland, but even they could not prevail against that island's conversion to Christianity.

King Caratacus

❧

Chief of the southern British Catuvellauni tribe, Caratacus formed the first line of resistance to the Emperor Claudius's forces when they invaded Britain in AD 43. The 40,000 Roman infantry were more than equal to the task of defeating Caratacus's men, many of whom would have gone into battle completely naked, with only small wooden shields for protection.

Nevertheless, it took two days for the Romans to consider the battle won and begin their push inland, up the River Thames. Caratacus (his name being the Roman version of the Celtic Caradoc) managed to escape with a sizable number of men and make his way to Wales. It was there that he established a new stronghold from which he fought a guerrilla war for another eight years.

He was aided in his resistance by local tribes, and it was with their help that Caratacus formed the army that confronted Roman forces near the River Severn in AD 51. Once more defeated, Caratacus escaped north and sought the hospitality of the Brigantes tribe. It was their queen, Cartimandua, who betrayed him to the Romans.

Taken in chains to Rome, where he was marched in triumphant procession, Caratacus is reputed to have asked his captors: "Why, when you have all this, do you envy us our poor huts?"

Granted his life and freedom by the Emperor Claudius, Caratacus is believed to have ended his days in Rome, a model citizen.

Hadrian's Wall

❖

In AD 122, during his only visit to Britain, the Emperor Hadrian learned of the problems his generals were experiencing in Scotland and ordered the construction of the fortified wall that now bears his name. This remarkable feat of engineering took eight years to complete, using local stone at its eastern end and millions of tons of turf in the west.

While Hadrian's Wall did act as a deterrent against marauding Scots, its chief purpose was that of frontier checkpoint. It was built, repaired and defended by soldiers, most of them "foreign" or non-Roman auxiliaries once the original soldier/builders left to perform active duty elsewhere.

Fortified gateways – now called "milecastles" – were built into the wall, each with living quarters for occupying troops. Watchtowers were placed at equal distances between each pair of milecastles, although the most their occupants observed was the comings and goings of traders, all paying a toll as they passed through.

An inhospitable location in winter, Hadrian's Wall was the last place that soldiers from Italy or Gaul wanted to be sent, and a number of letters home have been found, pleading for relatives to send them warm socks and underwear! There is ample evidence that soldiers kept their own livestock and bought locally produced fruit and vegetables to supplement their diet of meat, eggs and freshly caught fish and oysters from the sea.

No hell on earth, then, even if it was the final frontier...

A Scottish Ambush

❦

An old Scottish tale recounts how, in the fog-enshrouded dark of a winter's night, Roman soldiers heard shouted taunts and an invitation to fight from a lone voice on the Scottish side of Hadrian's Wall. The watch commander promptly sent three men out into the darkness with orders to sort out this silly wee man. After a confused muddle of noise, the Scots voice resumed his taunting, asking if that was the best Romans could do and questioning their manhood.

Enraged, the commander ordered ten more of his guard into action. As before, once the sounds of fighting died away, the lone voice returned, this time suggesting that no Roman soldier knew who his true father was – or words to that effect.

This time a fully-armed detachment of twenty Romans headed out into the fog. Eventually, after another fearful fight had subsided, a lone survivor crawled back to the watch commander's position, battered and bloody.

"What happened, soldier?" he was asked.

"It was a trap, sir," the man groaned. "There were two of 'em!"

Christianity in Britain

❧

As growing numbers of Romans converted to Christianity during the 2nd and 3rd centuries, it was inevitable that the young religion would find its way to Britain. As in Rome, early British Christians were subjected to vicious persecution. The most notable of these, perhaps, was Alban, a Roman citizen of Verulamium who was martyred for his beliefs in AD 304. The modern cathedral city of St Albans was named for him.

When Emperor Constantine became a Christian only eight years later, the Roman Empire as a whole followed suit.

The most spectacular early conversions were those achieved by St Patrick in Ireland during the 5th century. Son of a Romanized British Christian family, he was kidnapped by Irish raiders and spent six years in captivity before escaping. Returning to Ireland some years later, Patrick traveled far and wide converting and baptizing Irish chiefs and their families, establishing churches and opening the way for others to carry Christianity to Scotland.

England was not converted en-masse until the late 6th century when missionaries under St Augustine began work on the Anglo-Saxon hierarchy, and it was they who finally drove out the last vestiges of old Celtic religious beliefs.

Celtic artistic tradition was to live on in the illuminated manuscripts created by Christian monks during the next four or five hundred years, including the remarkable Book of Kells (which is now housed in Ireland) and the Lindisfarne Gospels, gathered in the monastery situated on the Northumbrian island of that name.

Decline and Fall

✦

By the middle of the 5th century, the Roman Empire was breaking up. Suffering from a succession of weak emperors and repeated attacks from so-called "barbarians," Rome was in no position to govern or defend its distant provinces – and Britain was more distant than most.

Although the Roman army had tried to defend Britain by building forts on the southern and eastern coasts and using ships to repel pirate raids in the North Sea and the Channel, a simultaneous invasion by three northern British tribes – the Picts, Scots and Allocotti – saw the Romans lose control of the south in 367.

Rome sent in a new commander, Theodosius, to restore order. In 383 another British-based general, Magnus Maximus, declared himself emperor and withdrew most of the army. Fifteen years later barbarian tribes once more invaded Britain, and by 406 so many Germanic invaders had infiltrated Gaul (France) that Britain was effectively cut off from

Rome. The last Roman soldiers were ordered out of
Britain and into Gaul.

In 410 Emperor Honorius wrote an open letter to
all British cities advising them that they were alone
and would have to defend themselves from now on.

2
The Dark Ages
501-1100

❧

This period owes its name to the notion that European civilization was suspended when the Roman Empire fell – an oversimplification which does not take into account that its former citizens now boasted societies with complex legal and governmental systems acquired from the Romans. While some tribes were undeniably barbaric in their treatment of those they conquered, they were not barbarians in the true sense.

The first outsiders to arrive in Britain after the Romans left did so at the invitation of a king who needed help against the Picts and Scots. These mercenaries were Angles, Saxons and Jutes – mostly from northwest Germany and Denmark.

Mutiny by these mercenaries led to a state of civil

war. The Britons retreated west, halting the Saxon advance only in AD 500 when a British warlord known as Ambrosius Aurelianus was victorious at the Battle of Mons Badonicus. It was during his period that the first legends of King Arthur appeared. The Saxons also advanced west of the Pennine mountain range in northern England, and north into the Scottish region of Lothian.

England became a leading European centre of scholarship, with Northumbria the jewel in its crown. It was there that the Venerable Bede, the theological historian, compiled his chronicles of early Britain. It is thought that *Beowulf*, the epic Saxon saga and the greatest poem in Old English, was also written during this time.

King Arthur

✤

One of the greatest figures of legend, King Arthur may not have actually existed. Many believe that the military exploits of the real-life Romano-British warlord, Ambrosius Aurelianus, were grafted on to age-old Celtic myths to give beleaguered Britons an inspirational super-hero.

A man of great chivalry, Arthur reputedly founded the order of knights who gathered around a great Round Table before embarking on often-dangerous quests. There is a round table on display in the great hall in Winchester (former capital of Wessex), but this is undeniably a fake. Arthur's fabled castle, Camelot, is most strongly linked with the Celtic hill-fort at Tintagel, Cornwall.

Guided by the wizard Merlin, who is also a composite of other Irish, Breton and Welsh druidic figures, Arthur is said to have married the beautiful Guinevere, who then fell in love with his friend and chief champion, Lancelot. Magic plays a large role in Arthur's story, including his finding the magic sword,

Excalibur (another repeated Celtic legend), which was reclaimed by the mysterious Lady of the Lake when Arthur died in battle. It was Celtic tradition to dispose of weapons by offering them to water-gods.

Fact or fiction, the legend of Arthur is a great story, all the same.

The Vikings

❧

The Vikings began their expeditions from Denmark, Norway and Sweden in the late 8th century, sailing in light, flat-bottomed boats which were capable of crossing wide expanses of open sea and traveling up-river to inland sites. Not all Vikings were warriors – many were farmers seeking more and better land.

Monasteries and coastal towns were their first targets, but they also attacked cities like Paris and Cologne. They visited the Mediterranean as far east as the Holy Land and Turkey. In Britain they settled in Ireland, north and west Scotland, the Isle of Man, and northeastern England, taking local wives and raising families. They also acquired Normandy in 911, gifted to them by King Rollo of France.

Vikings settled Iceland, Greenland and visited the east coast of North America – more than 300 years before Christopher Columbus "discovered" that continent. Swedish Vikings established trading posts in the Russian cities of Kiev and Novrogod, acquiring goods from as far away as China. Others fought with

Arab tribes, while the Norman Vikings colonized the southern mainland of Italy and the island of Sicily.

Vikings wrote in stick-like letters (called runes), which were carved on wood, metal or stone, and brought a number of their own words to the British language – most especially the names of their gods which became days of the week: Tyr (Tuesday), Woden (Wednesday), Thor (Thursday) and Frigg (Friday).

The Rise of Mercia

✦

As England's fate continued to be decided by force of arms, the 7th century saw the rise of Mercia. Originally a small kingdom in the northwest Midlands, by 628 it had absorbed all the peoples of the Severn Valley along the Welsh border. With Northumbria busy battling the Picts in the north, Mercian kings – most notably Offa – increased their powers. Before his death in 796 Offa was able to order the construction of the massive dyke which bears his name. It had the dual purpose of marking the boundary between his kingdom and Wales, and of securing Mercia from sudden Welsh attacks.

Offa was succeeded by a number of kings who lacked his strength and wisdom. That, combined with increasing numbers of attacks on East Anglia and northern England by Danish Vikings (whose Scandinavian cousins now held northern Scotland), led to a decline in Mercia's power and its union with Wessex. In 886, Alfred, the king of Wessex, was acclaimed as lord of all the English who had not fallen under Danish rule.

Offa of Mercia

❧

Under Offa, the Mercians were able to conquer and dominate most English provinces south of the River Humber. By 785 Offa was powerful enough for the Frankish king, Charlemagne (Charles the Great), to view him as an equal, hoping that Offa's daughter would marry his own son, also called Charles.

Instead, Offa married her to King Aethelred of Northumbria in 794, a shrewd move which led to a reduction in hostilities. Although miffed by this slight, Charlemagne initiated new, mutually beneficial trade deals with Offa.

Offa also befriended Pope Adrian I who allowed him to increase his control over the English church. By establishing an archbishopric in Lichfield (in Staffordshire) Offa freed the Mercian church from the authority of Canterbury, which was controlled by his enemies in the kingdom of Kent.

Besides the permanent personal memorial of the great earthworks called Offa's Dyke, Offa gained his place in history by establishing a new form of coinage bearing the sovereign's name and title, as well as the name of the mint responsible for the quality of those coins. Offa's principles governing coinage would be employed in England for many centuries.

Alfred the Great

❧

Alfred's appointment followed his emergence as a brilliant strategist and fighter. His reign was notable for strong internal government, a reorganizing of finances and his creation of the first state-sponsored navy. A scholar of note, Alfred encouraged the publication of many important books, not least being the seminal *Anglo-Saxon Chronicle*.

Succeeded by his son, Edward, in 899 Alfred's success in curbing Danish power was continued by his heir. In 912 Edward began a well-planned advance by Wessex against Danelaw (the name given to Danish territories), aided by his sister Aethelflaed, queen of Mercia. Together they regained Essex, East Anglia and the east Midlands. Faced by invasions by Norsemen from Ireland in the northwest and Northumbria, Edward built castles in Thelwall and Manchester. Within a year he'd received the invaders' submission, as well as that of the Northumbrians, the Scots and the Strathclyde Welsh. Even so, Norse kings would reign intermittently at York until 954.

Renewed Viking attacks weakened England and in 1013 King Ethelred accepted Sweyn, king of Denmark, as sovereign. He was succeeded by King Canute, and under his rule a number of English lords were promoted to powerful positions in court. Canute also invaded Scotland in 1031 and confirmed his Christianity by making a pilgrimage to Rome.

Scotland: Birth of a Nation

❧

During the Dark Ages Scotland was busy reshaping itself to face the future. While Vikings held much of the far north and northwest, Pictavia and Dalradia were established north of the Rivers Clyde and Forth by the Christian Scots who had come from Ireland. Welsh Britons colonized the Scottish southwest, which they called Strathclyde, while the Angles took the southeast and named it Bernicia.

The two northern kingdoms united in 843 under Kenneth MacAlpin, renaming themselves Scotland. By 1018 Kenneth's successors had absorbed the rest of the lands north of Hadrian's Wall to create the nation we know today. In 1040 Malcolm II's son, Duncan, was killed in a battle at Bothnagowan with a chief called Macbeth, who ruled for 17 years before being slain, in turn, by Duncan's son, Malcolm III.

In 1072 this Malcolm (who married a Saxon, Margaret, who was later named a saint) swore allegiance to the new English king, William the Conqueror, even though he continued raiding

England. It was during one such raid, in 1093, that he was killed.

King Canute

❧

Surrounded by sycophants, Canute was famously told on one occasion that his authority was so complete, and his power so overwhelming, that he could even order the sea to turn back.

Aware that this was utter nonsense, Canute announced his intention of proving his court creeps wrong. He and his entourage headed for the seashore where the king solemnly commanded the incoming tide to retreat.

It didn't, of course, and Canute's boots were duly soaked. It is not recorded what happened to the toadying courtiers, but as Canute had a fearsome reputation for severe retribution against all who offended him . . .

A Broken Promise

❧

In 1042 Edward the Confessor (a pious man who would later be named a saint) assumed the English throne, made an uneasy peace with Scotland and Wales and expanded England's trade with France. He also, fatally, promised Count William of Normandy the English throne when he died. There was another claimant, however – Harold of Wessex. Despite swearing that he would honor Edward's pledge to William, Harold seized the English crown when Edward died.

Securing papal support for his claim, in 1066 William's army set sail from France. Harold – his forces weakened by continued fighting against Danish troops in the north – met him in battle near Hastings, on the Kent coast, and was killed, reputedly by an arrow in his eye.

The Norman Conquest had begun and William the Conqueror was the new king of England.

One In The Eye

❦

The night before Harold's army met William the Conqueror's troops in the Battle of Hastings, the English king made a tour of the camp to raise morale. A group of infantry staged an exhibition of their swordsmanship for his approval, after which a number of archers stepped forward and asked if they could show him just how quickly they could fire their bows, reload and shoot again.

Harold agreed, but was appalled by the clumsiness of one man. Slow and ungainly, he was also clearly unable to shoot straight, his arrows flying off at wild angles.

Taking their commander aside, Harold told him: "I'd leave that one out tomorrow, if I were you. He could have someone's eye out!"

William the Conqueror

✦

Crowned King William I of England on Christmas Day 1066, William the Conqueror was Duke of Normandy and so owed allegiance to the French king. Confronted by resistance in the north and east of England, William ruthlessly pursued all rebels, taking their lands and gifting them either to his followers or a church now run by French bishops and priests.

William also encouraged French craftsmen and merchants to move to England and transformed society with the introduction of the feudal system. Under this regime, people held land in exchange for services to the king or his officers. Barons who'd been given estates paid annual taxes and were obliged to provide William with knights and soldiers to help him maintain an efficient army.

Under William, the Normans built many imposing castles and cathedrals. French monks and nuns established communities in England and Wales, and French became the language of the ruling class. In

1085 William carried out the first census of his extensive lands. Known as the Domesday Book, it remains an invaluable snapshot of a nation that was changing more dramatically than at any time before or since.

3
The Middle Ages
1100–1460

A remarkable period, the Middle Ages were marked in Britain – as was the rest of Europe – by war, intrigue, revolt, pestilence and more war. In the midst of this turmoil the boundaries of the known world were expanded greatly, not only by the explorations of adventurers and traders but also in the invention, in Germany around 1440, of the first printing press.

The Normans had to repel and subdue substantial rebellions in Wales, Scotland and Ireland (which they did with maximum force and brutality) and wage an almost constant war in France to hold on to Normandy. The rise to power of the Plantagenets from 1154 gave Britain a number of all-powerful but often weak kings and led, inevitably, to further rebellion, the drawing up of Magna Carta in 1215 to give the people some say in the decision-making process, and the first parliament in London.

The downside of international travel came in the form of the Black Death, a plague brought from the Far East which decimated the population of Britain and Europe. This in turn led to the Peasants' Revolt of 1381 and the first stirrings of a break with the Catholic Church in Rome, in part inspired by the first translation of the Bible into English.

By the end of the Middle Ages Scotland was an independent and increasingly powerful player on the political stage. Wales and Ireland continued to be governed by England, although the Irish managed to restrict English control to a relatively small area around Dublin known as The Pale. To this day uncontrollable people are described as being "beyond The Pale."

As this period drew to a close, the shape of English history was changed forever when the rival houses of York and Lancaster embarked on a bloody and divisive war (the War of the Roses) to win the throne. It ended early in 1486 with the marriage of the Lancastrian Henry VII to Elizabeth of York. The Tudor dynasty had begun.

William Rufus and Henry I

❧

William the Conqueror had three sons – Robert, William Rufus and Henry. Robert was given charge of family estates in Normandy and when William Sr died in 1087 it was Rufus who became William II of England. He was aware, however, that his brother Henry also wanted the crown.

William II's own ambition was to wrest control of Normandy from Robert, a dream he achieved in 1096 when Robert decided to mount a crusade to the Holy Land. He raised the necessary funds by mortgaging Normandy to Rufus for 10,000 marks! Imposing heavy taxes on his subjects to raise this, Rufus saw his popularity plummet and a growing number of barons go over to his brother Henry's side.

In 1100, William Rufus was "accidentally" killed while hunting in the New Forest. Henry (conveniently a member of that party), galloped to Winchester, seized the treasury and was acclaimed king the following day.

Henry I was, all things considered, a just and

even-handed sovereign. He managed to gain control of Normandy and began a long war with Louis VI of France. He also married off his only legitimate son, William, to Matilda, daughter of the Duke of Anjou.

Henry's plans for William died with his son's death by drowning in 1120. He promptly arranged the marriage of his brother's daughter (another Matilda, by now married to the German emperor, Henry V) to the 14-year-old Geoffrey of Anjou, 11 years her junior. Geoffrey and Matilda produced three children – a situation guaranteed to create chaos when Henry died of a heart attack in 1135.

It did. England and Wales were pitched into 19 years of civil war as supporters of rival claimants (Matilda and Stephen, Henry's nephew) fought it out. Along the way Stephen won the support of King David of Scotland by granting him control of Carlisle and Doncaster. By the time Henry II, the first Plantagenet king of England, succeeded to the throne in 1154 the nation was in sore need of a strong and decisive ruler. Henry would prove equal to the task.

The Crusades

❖

Christians had traveled unmolested in pilgrimage from Europe to Palestine ("the Holy Land") since the 2nd century, even after Muslim Arabs conquered the region. When Turks began persecuting Christians towards the end of the 11th century, Pope Urban II called on Christian leaders to reclaim the Holy Land. Because knights who answered Urban's call wore large crosses on their chests, they became known as Crusaders, a term inspired by the Spanish word *cruzada* which means "marked with the Cross." There would be nine full-scale Crusades during the next 200 years before the Muslims succeeded in throwing Christians out of the Holy Land.

The first Crusade was led by the unpromisingly named Walter the Penniless and Peter the Hermit. It never reached Palestine. A more disciplined force later captured Jerusalem and established four Christian kingdoms. Muslim leaders were aided in their struggle to evict these invaders by rivalries between these kingdoms.

The legend of the Pied Piper of Hamelin may have its roots in the ill-fated Children's Crusade of 1212 which saw thousands of youngsters lured away from their homes. Many were sold into slavery while others simply gave up and returned home. None of them are known to have reached Palestine.

Henry II and Thomas à Becket

❖

First and greatest of the three Angevin – from Anjou – kings of England, Henry II came to the throne in 1154 as owner of vast properties, power and influence. Besides Anjou, he inherited the French territories of Maine, Touraine, Brittany, Normandy and Aquitaine. In all, Henry's holdings in France were bigger than the French king's. He also inherited England and Wales.

He would reign for 34 years, the last 11 of which were spent battling with his two sons, Richard and John, the French king, Louis, and plots hatched by his wife, Eleanor. He subdued Eleanor by retiring her to a genteel imprisonment and exile.

Attempting to reinstate the close relationship between church and state established by the Norman kings, Henry installed his friend and chancellor, Thomas à Becket, as Archbishop of Canterbury in 1162, only to see him become a militant defender of church rights. Two years later Henry brought charges against Thomas for alleged embezzlement. Thomas fled to France and was only reconciled with Henry in 1170, after the king's eldest son, also named Henry, had been crowned king-in-waiting by the Archbishop of York, not Canterbury.

When Becket excommunicated the clergy who'd taken part in the York coronation, an exasperated Henry reputedly uttered the fateful words ("Who will rid me of this meddlesome priest?") which inspired four knights to sail for England and murder Thomas in Canterbury Cathedral. Public outrage forced Henry to disclaim responsibility for the assassination and promise reconciliation with the church. Thomas à Becket was soon after named a saint.

In 1183, when Henry's declared heir died, the question of succession renewed the rivalry of his surviving sons, Richard and John, and their attacks on him. Richard was aided by the new French king, Philip II Augustus. Henry died an embittered old man in 1189, knowing that neither of his sons were fit to succeed him.

Richard the Absent Lion

❧

While he's gone into legend as a romantic hero and brave warrior (hence his nickname, "Lionheart"), Richard was an unpopular and weak king whose ten-year reign was spent mostly in the Holy Land and Europe, leaving England to be run by a committee.

Waging war and carrying out crusades was an expensive business and the imposition of punishing taxes to fund the king's adventures was only one factor that enabled Richard's brother, John, to find supporters for a revolt. Richard's allies — with help from Queen Eleanor — put down John's challenge. Strangely, Richard forgave John and promised him the succession.

Captured and held to ransom by Leopold of Austria on his way back from the Holy Land, Richard raised most of the 150,000 marks demanded with further high taxes. A growing number of English subjects also refused to serve in France. When Richard died in 1199 (he was involved in the siege of a French city at the time), John inherited a realm which was nearly bankrupt and disastrously divided by rivalry.

Robin Hood

❧

Forget all the tales of derring-do you've ever heard, read or seen concerning Robin Hood, his battles with the Sheriff of Nottingham or his brave band of brigands in fetching tights and green tunics. All of that is based on a "pedigree" created by an imaginative 18th-century antiquary.

The first mention of Robin comes from 14th-century ballads and may be linked to the Peasants' Revolt of 1381, when there was a demand for a golden hero. The theme of a courageous renegade thumbing his nose at those charged with stopping commoners from hunting in the king's forests would have appealed to peasants subjected to the same laws. In these ballads, Robin's adventures took place in Yorkshire, not Nottinghamshire.

Not until the 16th century did Robin's "aristocratic" background enter the legends, to be embellished by later novelists, playwrights and screenwriters. Sadly, there has never been any evidence that Robin Hood ever existed in real life. Nor, alas, did Maid Marian.

Bad King John

✦

One of the most reviled figures in English history, King John's principal burden was the widespread resentment that had built up against his father and brother, Richard. Lacking both men's military skills, John soon lost all his lands in France, only holding on to the Channel Islands. He also fell out with the Pope, who excommunicated him in 1209.

In 1212, John was confronted by the first of what would be many rebellions by his barons. He solved this by arranging a reconciliation with the Pope, accepting the pontiff's choice of archbishop of Canterbury, and reinstating exiled clergy to their posts.

Organizing a coalition of rulers in Germany and the Low Countries to assist him in a failed attempt to overthrow the French king, John began raising the costs of that doomed exercise by imposing the highest taxes ever levied in England, compounding his mistake by charging the barons an inheritance tax.

This move sparked the biggest revolt yet and in

1215 a gathering of disgruntled barons presented John with Magna Carta (literally "the Great Charter") in a meadow at Runnymede, west of London. This document not only protected its authors against the king's arbitrary disregard of feudal rights but gave some measure of legal protection for all freemen by guaranteeing them judgment by peers or the law of the land. Magna Carta thus established the notion that the realm was a community that should be governed by representatives of that community, not by the king alone.

Although the later 1225 version of Magna Carta was the one which really gave knights a voice at national level through a parliament, John's reluctant signature on the 1215 original was enough to put off a full-scale civil war until he died a year later.

Henry III and the Barons

✤

A babe in arms when he ascended to the throne in 1216, Henry III would manage to reign for 56 years despite spending much of it at war with various baronial factions. Many of these rebellions were caused by Henry's marriage in 1236 to Eleanor of Provence and the arrival in the English court of many of her Savoyard relations. A titanic struggle for supremacy began.

Matters came to a head in 1258. Henry suffered reversals in Wales and was forced to agree to the creation of a national committee. Additionally, Parliament would meet three times a year, not merely when the king chose to order a session.

In 1260 this arrangement began to break down. There were divisions among the king's principal opponents, the Earl of Gloucester and Simon de Montfort, Earl of Leicester, who was also Henry's brother-in-law. As de Montfort's strength grew, Henry arranged to have their dispute arbitrated by Louis IX of France. The resulting verdict was so favorable to Henry that de Montfort refused to accept it and launched a full-scale offensive.

After winning a resounding victory at Lewes, Sussex, de Montfort called a parliament in 1265 – the first gathering at which representatives of English boroughs sat alongside knights of the shires. Shortly after, Prince Edward rallied loyal royalists, including the Welsh lords. In August, Edward's army met de Montfort's force at Evesham and the rebel earl was killed.

Henry spent the rest of his reign settling the problems created by de Montfort's revolt, but by 1270 England was sufficiently peaceful for Prince Edward to depart on a crusade to the Holy Land. He did not return to claim his throne until 1274, two years after his father's death.

Edward I

Like his father, Edward I was to find the repeated revolts of his Welsh subjects an expensive diversion. Worse, he found himself embroiled in Scottish disputes which brought him into confrontations with, among others, the legendary William "Braveheart" Wallace and Robert the Bruce. Although Wallace would be defeated, captured and executed, Bruce would seize the Scottish crown, outlive Edward and continue to frustrate his son.

Edward's reign began with him applying a duty on exported wool products to pay his crusade debts. He also borrowed heavily from Italian bankers, and it may have been as a result of their lobbying that he ordered the expulsion of all Jews from the kingdom in 1290.

Welsh opposition was initially led by Llywelyn ap Gruffudd, prince of Gwynedd. Edward's victory over Llywelyn in 1277 saw him win undisputed title over much of north Wales. Within five years, however, Welsh resentment led to a new revolt by Llywelyn's younger brother, David. Edward mounted another war during which Llywelyn was killed. David was captured and executed. Major castles built in Flint and Rhuddlan after the first war were now supplemented by grand fortresses in Conway, Caernarvon and Harlech. The last of Edward's castles was built in Beaumaris, on the island of Anglesey, after a further Welsh rebellion began in 1294.

Edward in Scotland

❧

Edward I first intervened in Scotland's complex succession disputes in 1291 when there were no fewer than 13 claimants to the throne left vacant by the deaths of Alexander III (in a riding accident) and his young daughter, Margaret, who'd been promised in marriage to Edward's son. The two best-placed claimants were John de Balliol and Robert the Bruce. A court voted in favor of Balliol, who duly swore loyalty to Edward. In 1295, however, a Scottish baronial court made a treaty with France, with whom Edward was also in a state of constant conflict.

Victory over Balliol in 1296 was deceptively easy and in 1297 a fresh rebellion – led by William Wallace and Andrew Moray – led to a bitter year-long war which seemed won at the Battle of Falkirk, after which Wallace fled into hiding. Resistance continued until 1314, however, when Robert the Bruce – by now the Scottish king – defeated English forces at the battle of Bannockburn.

That situation, and many other headaches Edward

left as legacy of his reign, would give his son, Edward II, a hard row to hoe when he ascended to the English throne in 1307.

William Wallace

❖

The son of Sir Malcolm Wallace, a Renfrew landowner, William Wallace was 26 years old when Edward I deposed and imprisoned the Scottish king, John de Balliol, in 1296. A year later Wallace led a band of 30 men who attacked and burned Lanark, killing its English sheriff. He then launched assaults on English garrisons and scored a major victory at Stirling before invading the English counties of Northumberland and Cumberland.

Knighted and proclaimed guardian of Scotland on his return, it was not until July 1298 that Wallace's forces had to face an English army led by Edward himself, who'd been away fighting in France. That confrontation, at Falkirk, saw Wallace's spearmen defeated by Edward's archers and cavalry. His military reputation ruined, Wallace resigned his guardianship.

It is thought that he traveled to France before becoming a guerrilla leader in Scotland. In August 1305 he was arrested near Glasgow, taken to London and publicly hanged, disemboweled, beheaded and quartered. The divided parts of his body were returned to Scotland and displayed as a dreadful warning to all would-be rebels. One of those who would view this barbaric act as a challenge was Robert the Bruce, and in 1306 he would raise the rebellion that eventually won Scotland's independence.

Robert the Bruce

❧

Heir of an Anglo-Norman family which settled in Scotland in the early 12th century, Robert the Bruce was born in 1274. His unsuccessful bid to become Scottish king in 1290 saw him embark on a duplicitous political career during which he first swore allegiance to King Edward, then supported William Wallace. He switched sides once more just before Edward defeated Wallace at Falkirk.

Bruce's rise to the title of King Robert I in 1306 followed the murder of his main rival, John "The Red" Comyn, nephew of John de Balliol. Edward I viewed Bruce as a traitor and defeated him in battle twice that year, executing three of his brothers. Robert hid on the remote island of Rathlin, off the north Irish coast.

After his supporters conquered Galloway, Douglasdale and most of the eastern borders, in 1314 Bruce captured Edinburgh. On June 24 that year he scored his final conclusive battle with the army of Edward II at Bannockburn, near Stirling.

During the 15 years of his reign Bruce seized all lands and titles of nobles who remained loyal to the English crown and rebuilt a royal administration that had been more or less suspended since 1296. By the time of his death in 1329 (maybe of leprosy), Scotland was functioning efficiently as an autonomous state.

According to tradition, Robert the Bruce's heart was buried at Melrose Abbey, an attempt to take it to the Holy Land failing when the man charged with this mission, Sir James Douglas, was killed en route to Palestine.

Edward II

❧

A notoriously weak king, Edward II's early reign was marked by his inability to tackle either the problem of the £200,000 budget deficit his father left or the Scottish war now being led by Robert the Bruce. He had none of his father's strengths and rejected the company of a loyal ruling class in favor of Piers Gaveston, a Gascon knight with whom he had a homosexual relationship. Edward's father had tried to quash this affair by exiling Gaveston. Edward II recalled his friend to England, gave him the earldom of Cornwall and arranged his marriage to Margaret de Clare, sister of the Earl of Gloucester.

The middle years of Edward's reign were marked by his struggle with Thomas, 2nd Earl of Lancaster, his cousin. Lancaster consistently blocked Edward's political initiatives, arranged the capture and execution of Piers Gaveston in 1312 and rose to dominance after Edward's disastrous defeat at Bannockburn.

In 1321 Welsh nobles moved against two of

Edward's favorites, a father and son both named Hugh Despenser. Parliament ordered their exile, but the Despensers soon returned to take Edward's side in a short civil war with Lancaster. The victorious Edward had Lancaster executed and murdered many of his supporters.

The final period of Edward's rule saw the Despensers returned to power and the treasury restored to a healthy £60,000 balance, thanks to widespread corruption, and in 1327 Edward's estranged queen, Isabella, launched an invasion led by her lover, Roger Mortimer, later to become Earl of March.

With the support of London's put-upon citizens, the Despensers were executed, Edward's government overthrown and the king imprisoned. Edward was deposed, forced to abdicate in favor of his son, who was crowned Edward III. After two attempts to free him, Edward II was killed at Berkeley Castle. His murderers reputedly effected the bisexual king's demise by impaling him on a red-hot poker . . .

Edward III, "King of France"

❧

Only five years old when he became king, Edward III's realm was initially governed by his mother, Isabella, and her lover, Mortimer, although his nominal guardian was Henry, Earl of Lancaster. It was he who signed the treaty which made Scotland an independent realm – a settlement Edward would break 11 years later. His popularity soared when he revived England's favorite sport of warring with France.

Edward became his own man when he captured Mortimer and had him executed. In 1330 Edward moved against David II, the young Scottish king, replacing him with Edward Balliol. David fled to France, returning in 1341 after Balliol's puppet regime ran out of allies.

Disputes with Philip VI of France over England's title to Gascony gave Edward the excuse to invade France. After two unsuccessful campaigns Edward simply assumed the French title, so beginning the instability which would become known as The

Hundred Years' War. Until 1801 every English sovereign also termed him/herself King (or Queen) of France.

At home, Edward began the rebuilding of Windsor Castle and instituted the Order of the Garter, Britain's highest order of knighthood. The new phase of his French war began in 1346 when he – accompanied by his eldest son, Prince Edward ("The Black Prince," due to his distinctive armor) – fought his way to the gates of Paris. It was during this campaign that he defeated French forces in the battle of Crécy and forced the surrender of Calais. This port would be colonized and used as a base for future invasions.

Not even the widespread horror of the Black Death was allowed to spoil the pleasure of life at Edward's court, nor his continued attacks on the French and Scots. His war exploits were overshadowed by those of the Black Prince, however. In 1356 Edward's son defeated the new French king, John II, at Poitiers, forcing him to surrender so much territory that their treaty was repudiated by the French court. Edward was obliged to reinvade France.

His last attempt to lead an army into France was frustrated by storms in 1372, by which time his heir was in failing health (he would die before his father, in 1376) and the power base of John of Gaunt (his name being an Anglicization of his birthplace, the Belgian city of Ghent), the Duke of Lancaster, was proving the strongest in England. When Edward III died in 1377, the house of Lancaster stood ready to seize control.

The Black Death

❧

A form of bubonic plague, the Black Death got its name from the spots of blood which formed under the skin and turned black before its victims died. Earlier symptoms were the swelling of glands in the armpit and groin. Those afflicted lasted only a few hours before dying.

Responsible for the deaths of 25 million people in Europe – about a quarter of the population – the Black Death arrived in Europe from Asia in 1347, carried by fleas on rats which hitched rides on trading ships.

The first reported cases of the disease were in the Italian port of Genoa. It spread north and west rapidly, hitting Paris and London for the first time in 1348. Northern Russia and Scandinavia succumbed a year later. The only defense seemed to be complete isolation and some communities survived the worst of the Black Death's ravages by cutting themselves off from their neighbors.

Before the Black Death Europe boasted a surplus

of workers, so wages were kept low. Afterwards, a depleted workforce was able to demand greater reward for their labors. Attempts to hold wages down led to revolts across the continent and the decline of an already fractured feudal system.

Richard II

❧

The 22 years of Richard II's reign were fraught and volatile, not least because Edward III's grandson was only ten years old when he became king. England was governed by a "continual council" from which John of Gaunt – the most powerful member of the royal family – was excluded. Trouble was bound to follow.

It did. In 1381 attempts to speed up collection of an already unpopular poll tax sparked the Peasants' Revolt. Increased taxes were not the only bone of contention but they were enough for peasants in Kent and Essex to attack tax collectors, landlords (including wealthy churches) and lawyers. In June they marched on London, laid siege to John of Gaunt's palace and broke into the Tower of London to kill a number of officials.

Young Richard met the rebels at Smithfield where Wat Tyler, their leader, presented his demands, only to be run through and killed by the Lord Mayor's sword. Richard calmed the crowd by saying he'd agree to their terms. Once they departed, however, he reneged on his pledge.

Richard also faced unrest caused by the preachings of John Wycliffe, an Oxford scholar and priest whose followers, called Lollards, followed his teachings that a sinful man had no right to authority – including most kings, earls, priests, even the Pope himself. It was a heresy that would see Wycliffe expelled from Oxford into a solitary life in a Leicestershire village. That would not end his movement, whose effectiveness was aided by Lollards publishing the first copies of a Bible translated into English.

Richard had numerous fights with Parliament but gained widespread popular support by putting down a rebellion in Ireland. Following the death of his queen, Anne of Bohemia, he married the seven-year-old daughter of the French king to create a 20-year truce with the old enemy.

There would be no truce at home. When the Duke of Norfolk and Henry Bolingbroke, John of Gaunt's son, accused each other of treason, Richard banished them both. After Gaunt died in 1399, Richard seized his estates and set off for Ireland. Bolingbroke returned from exile, landing in Yorkshire and – gaining the support of the powerful Percy family – raised a huge force to help reclaim his father's land

and titles. By the time Richard returned from Ireland matters were out of his control. He surrendered to Bolingbroke without a fight and abdicated.

Four months later Richard II died in Pontefract Castle, reportedly starving himself to death as Bolingbroke was crowned King Henry IV.

Geoffrey Chaucer

❧

Best remembered for his comic verse masterpiece
The Canterbury Tales, which recounts the stories told
by a group of pilgrims as they journey from London to
the tomb of Thomas à Becket in Canterbury,
Geoffrey Chaucer spent a lifetime writing a vast
amount of other poetry and plays, some of which are
counted as the equal of William Shakespeare. These
include his epic poem *Troilus and Cressida*.

The son of a wealthy London vintner, Chaucer
elected to pursue a career as diplomat and court official, serving in various posts for Edward III, Richard
II and Henry IV. Under Richard II he was appointed
clerk of the king's works, with executive responsibility
for the repair and maintenance of buildings like the
Tower of London and Westminster Palace. He also
visited Flanders, France and Italy as a diplomatic
envoy.

His career was so hectic that it's hard to imagine
how Chaucer found time to write the hundreds of
works which bear his name. He died, aged 65, in

1400 having witnessed some great and bloody events. He wisely chose to avoid court intrigues either in real life or as the subject of any of his writings!

John Wycliffe

❧

In contrast to Chaucer, John Wycliffe allowed himself to be drawn into the 14th century's greatest controversy. Taken up by John of Gaunt to promote his opposition to the clergy, Wycliffe was pursued first by the church and then by the state when he extended his criticisms to include the king.

Born in Yorkshire, possibly in 1330, Wycliffe studied at Oxford University before becoming a priest. He became a doctor of divinity in 1372, and was appointed to the parish of Lutterworth, Leicestershire by Edward III two years later. Within three years he was facing the first of many hearings to silence him.

Wycliffe began supervising the translation of the Bible into English in 1380, laying plans for an order of preachers who would take it to the people. While it's impossible to say how much Wycliffe's views inspired the Peasants' Revolt a year later, there is no doubt he sympathized with their aims. One of those killed in the revolt was the Archbishop of Canterbury.

It was his successor who condemned Wycliffe at a church synod held in 1382. Wycliffe was ordered back to Lutterworth and although he continued to write prolifically in exile, he lived only two years more, his role as the first reformer of the English church a matter of historical record.

Henry IV

❖

Overthrowing a king is one guaranteed way to make yourself enemies, so Henry Bolingbroke could not have been surprised to be forced to spend the first half of his 12-year reign defending himself against a formidable array of adversaries.

His first task was to quash a conspiracy of Richard II's supporters early in 1400, only to face a new threat later that same year when Owain Glyndwr – a Welsh landowner who had once served with the forces of the new king – raised a rebellion against English rule in Wales. While Henry mounted a number of campaigns against Glyndwr during the next five years, it was his son, the later Henry V, who had greater success in regaining control over Wales.

Glyndwr allied himself with Henry Percy, Earl of Northumberland and his son, Sir Henry Percy, nick-named "Hotspur" – the same men who'd helped Bolingbroke's rebellion against Richard II! The Northumberland revolt ended in July 1403 when King Henry's forces defeated and killed Hotspur in battle near Shrewsbury. Two years later Henry nipped a new Northumberland plot in the bud by executing co-conspirators Thomas Mowbray, Duke of Norfolk, and Richard Scrope, Archbishop of York.

The worst of his political troubles apparently over, Henry fell prey to an illness which some believe was congenital syphilis. The last Northumberland insurrection – in 1408 – was quickly suppressed, and while Henry had to deal with constant Scottish border raids and dissuade the French from helping Owain Glyndwr, his final years were spent falling out with a son and heir who hated him for making an alliance with a French faction at war with Prince Henry's friends in Burgundy.

Henry became completely incapacitated late in 1412 and died some months later. He would leave his throne to a man who, though only briefly a king, would prove himself the most able warrior of his time.

Owain Glyndwr

❖

Descended from the princes of Powys, Owain Glyndwr (in English, Owen Glendower) led the last major military attempt by the Welsh to end English rule. Inheriting several estates in north Wales, he studied law in London before serving with the force raised by Henry Bolingbroke, the later Henry IV.

Discovering widespread poverty and corruption among the English authorities when he returned home, Glyndwr also found himself embroiled in a vicious feud with a neighbor, Reynold, Lord Grey of Ruthin. This sparked an uprising in north Wales that quickly spread into a nationwide struggle for independence. By 1404 Glyndwr controlled most of his homeland.

Titling himself the Prince of Wales, Glyndwr established a Welsh Parliament and began making his own domestic and foreign policies. In 1405, however, he suffered two defeats at the hands of Prince Henry and his English allies were crushed.

By 1409 Prince Henry had captured all of

Glyndwr's principal strongholds. Glyndwr continued to fight a guerrilla war until 1412, his cause hopelessly lost. While he died in 1412, his spirit lived on, to be revived in the resurgence of Welsh nationalism in the 19th and 20th centuries.

Henry V

❦

Succeeding to the throne in 1413 appears to have calmed Henry V down considerably. A notable hell-raiser in his youth, he switched his energies from the pursuit of wine, women, and Welshmen to ferocious fighting of the French – especially when news reached him that Charles VI of France (known impolitely to his long-suffering subjects as "Charles the Silly") had finally lost his always slender touch with reality.

Henry's greatest triumph came in 1415 at the Battle of Agincourt, not far from the French port of Boulogne, when ranks of English longbowmen overcame a far bigger force of French knights on horseback (who got bogged down in the mud) and crossbow archers who couldn't match the firepower of their English opponents.

Between 1417 and 1419 Henry captured all of Normandy, granting land and titles to English nobles and freemen. Seeking to consolidate his political position, Henry married Charles's daughter and assumed the title Regent of France. Charles's son, the Dauphin, refused to acknowledge Henry's claim to the French throne, nor to Henry's heirs succeeding him in perpetuity. Henry still had a French war on his hands.

He was not fated to enjoy a long and glorious reign, however. In 1422 – when he was only 35 years old – Henry caught dysentery during the seige of Meaux and died. Shortly after, the mentally challenged King Charles of France followed suit, leaving an almighty can of worms for Henry's son – the one-year-old Henry VI – to tackle as best he could.

A Call To Arms

❖

Once more unto the breach, dear friends, once more;
Or close the wall up with our English dead.
In peace there's nothing so becomes a man
As modest stillness and humility;
But when the blast of war blows in our ears,
Then imitate the action of the tiger:
Stiffen the sinews, conjure up the blood,
Disguise fair nature with hard-favour'd rage.
Then lend the eye a terrible aspect....

Dishonour not your mothers; now attest
That those whom you call'd fathers did beget you.
Be copy now to men of grosser blood,
And teach them how to war. And you, good yeomen,
Whose limbs were made in England, show us here
The mettle of your pasture; let us swear
That you are worthy of your breeding – which I doubt
    not;
For there is none of you so mean and base
That hath not noble lustre in your eyes.
I see you stand like greyhounds in the slips,
Straining upon the start. The game's afoot:
Follow your spirit; and upon this charge
Cry, "God for Harry! England and Saint George!"

William Shakespeare, *Henry V*
(Excerpt from Henry's speech before the
Battle of Harfleur, 1415)

Henry VI

✤

Although described as a generous and pious man, Henry VI's life and reign was marred by poor political judgment and recurring bouts of madness. This weakness made revolt and conspiracy inevitable, and the rival claims of stewardship made by the houses of Lancaster and York would explode into what is called The War of the Roses.

Until he reached manhood, Henry's realm (which included all of France) was governed by a council of nobles dominated by the Beaufort family. His army was capably led by his uncle, the Duke of Bedford, until his death in 1435, by which time the French uprising of the charismatic Joan of Arc had begun to recapture all territories won by Henry V. By 1453 the English could only claim Calais.

At the urging of the Earl of Suffolk, in 1445 Henry married Margaret of Anjou. She and Suffolk dominated the king – especially during the mental breakdowns he suffered in 1450 and 1455 when Richard, Duke of York, ruled England as protector.

Suffolk had negotiated a peace with France in 1444 but was made a scapegoat when that broke down two years later. He was killed while fleeing into exile. Edmund Beaufort, Duke of Somerset, replaced him as leader of the court party. It was he who managed the defeat of rebels led by Jack Cade who threatened London a few months later. Cade's rebels demanded better and less corrupt government and that Henry accept the counsel of his greatest rival, the Duke of York.

The War of the Roses is explained separately, but by 1461 the Yorkist cause owed its victory over the Lancastrians to victories won by Edward, Earl of March. Advancing his army into London on March 4, Edward was acclaimed king by the capital's citizens and soldiers. He allowed Henry VI to live, but had reason to rue his magnanimity in 1470 when the old king reclaimed his throne, forcing Edward to flee to Holland. He returned the following year, won decisive victories and ordered Henry VI's execution.

The War of the Roses

✤

Both the Yorkist and Lancastrian descendants of Edward III had some claim to the throne of Henry VI – who was head of the Lancastrian faction – and sought control of government. Henry's inadequacies and the opposition of his principal rival, Richard, Duke of York, combined with smaller local Yorkist-Lancastrian feuds and English military setbacks in France, made the outbreak of civil war inevitable. The Lancastrians favored a red rose as their emblem, the Yorkists a white rose.

Sent to Ireland as a royal lieutenant in 1446, the Duke of York returned to England in 1450 with an army of 4,000 men, determined to participate in the king's council and counter the machinations of Edmund Beaufort, Duke of Somerset, who'd assumed the council leadership. In 1454 York was appointed the king's protector when Henry's madness first struck. When he recovered a year later, Henry had a son, Edward, and York was no longer heir apparent.

Gathering forces in the north, York met the king's

Lancastrians in battle at St Albans and won. Somerset was captured and killed and a Yorkist regime established with York as constable of England and the Earl of Warwick as captain of Calais. Henry VI fell ill again in late 1455 and York resumed his post as protector until Henry's recovery early in 1456.

Hostilities resumed in 1459 when the Yorkists fled from a Lancastrian force at Ludford Bridge, but within a year the Yorkist earls of Warwick and Salisbury launched an attack on England from Calais. Henry VI was captured during a Yorkist victory at Northampton and the Duke of York claimed the throne as heir to Richard II. While Parliament considered his claim a regrouped Lancastrian force met York's troops at Wakefield. He was killed, as was Warwick a short while later, at St Albans.

The Yorkist cause was saved by Richard's son, Edward, Earl of March, in two decisive battles – at Mortimer's Cross and Towton Moor, early in 1461. It was he who ascended to the throne his father had so coveted.

Joan of Arc

✤

Born in 1412, this daughter of a French farmer believed herself guided by the voices of St Michael, St Margaret and St Catherine to drive the English from her homeland. She swore herself loyal to Charles, the Dauphin, in his fight against Henry VI. Joan convinced the Dauphin of her sincerity, the truth of her visions and predicted that he would be crowned king of France at Reims. Charles agreed to let the now-famous 16-year-old join forces laying seige to the English stronghold at Orléans.

Inspired by a vision, Joan named the time and place for a French offensive and they seized the fort. During the next two months she led the Dauphin's army to a number of notable victories and was present at the ceremony held in Reims on July 17, 1429 at which he was crowned Charles VII.

Impatient to take Paris, Joan was wounded in a skirmish. Charles ordered a retreat, retired to the Loire region and disbanded his army. That winter he ennobled Joan, her parents and brothers. An uneasy peace with enemy Burgundians ended in the spring of 1430. Joan embarked on a trip to rally support for Charles. On May 25 her party was attacked and she was captured.

A year later, on May 30, 1431, Joan was burned alive in the main public square of Rouen after a lengthy trial resulted in guilty verdicts on a range of charges for treason and heresy. Jeanne d'Arc (her French name) was canonized as a saint in 1920, still a potent symbol of French national pride.

Edward IV

✦

From 1461 (when he overthrew Henry VI to become king) to 1470, Edward IV's reign was turbulent, not least because of the ploys and intrigues which beset him. Lancastrian resistance continued in the north-east and Wales, while France and Burgundy – allies of his mother, Margaret of Anjou – also remained a threat. Of greatest concern, however, was the end of his relationship with Richard "The Kingmaker" Neville, Earl of Warwick. Once Edward's staunchest friend, he allied himself with the king's young brother George, Duke of Clarence and – through the machinations of Louis XI of France – joined Queen Margaret's successful plot to depose Edward in 1470.

Within a year Edward had returned from Holland, thanks in no small part to the help he received from his brother-in-law, Charles the Bold of Burgundy. With Henry IV safely executed, Edward was able to enjoy a further 12 years on the throne, his popularity ensured by the fact that his personal wealth was so great that he had no need of higher taxes or subsidies and called Parliament only six times.

Edward died in 1483, aged 40 and worn out, it's said, by the sexual excesses of a debauched life. He left two legitimate sons, Edward and Richard, to the protection of his brother, Richard, Duke of Gloucester – a bad mistake. Richard placed both boys in the Tower of London and set about eliminating anyone who opposed him – including Lord Hastings, who'd sent word to Richard of Edward IV's death and warned him against the queen's party. His reward? Accused of treason and executed!

The day after the date set for Edward V's coronation, Parliament unanimously adopted a petition demanding that Richard be named king. He accepted with alacrity and, on July 6, 1483, was crowned Richard III. He elected to take his oath in English, the first sovereign to do so.

Richard III

❧

Although he was accepted because of his undoubted abilities, the honeymoon of Richard III's short reign lasted only a few months. It ended when news spread that his young nephews were dead. As no one was ever accused of their murder, it stood to reason that Richard had either ordered their deaths or conspired to have them killed.

Whatever the truth, Richard's suddenly villainous reputation obscured the fact that he was proving an able monarch, introducing legislation against corruption and greater protection for English merchants and craftsmen.

He managed to subdue a rebellion in 1483, but in the summer of 1485 found himself facing a far greater threat. When Henry Tudor – the sole male claimant to Lancastrian ancestry and the English throne – landed at Milford Haven, in the Welsh county of Pembrokeshire, most of Richard's supporters deserted him. Outflanked, outmaneuvered and outmanned by Henry Tudor's army, Richard was defeated and killed at the Battle of Bosworth Field, near Leicester, on August 22.

William Caxton

❖

Born around 1422 in Kent, William Caxton was apprenticed to Robert Large, a merchant who became Lord Mayor of London in 1439. When Large died two years later, Caxton moved to Bruges, heart of the European wool trade. During the next 30 years he became a prosperous and influential member of the Flanders and Holland trading community. In 1470 he joined the service of Margaret, Duchess of Burgundy, possibly as financial adviser.

His interests increasingly turning to literature, in 1469 Caxton began to learn the art of printing in Cologne, where he lived until late 1472. In his epilogue to his first translation (*The Recuyell of the Historyes of Troye*, the first ever book in English) Caxton recounted how his "pen became worn, his hand weary, his eye dimmed" while copying his text – hence his interest in printing.

In 1474 Caxton established his first press in Bruges, but returned to London in 1476 to set up shop in Westminster. Between then and his death in

1491, William Caxton produced close on 100 books, 24 of them his own translations of foreign works, and one of them Sir Thomas Malory's epic poem, *Morte d'Arthur*, the first reawakening of the Arthurian legend.

4
The Tudors
1485–1603

Henry VII

There was nothing about Henry VII which suggested that he would make any greater mark on history than his immediate predecessors, that he would reign for 24 years, nor that he would found a Tudor dynasty that would last for 118 years. His claim to the throne was pretty shaky. His Lancastrian blood was tainted twice over by illegitimacy: on his mother's side from a liaison between John of Gaunt and Katherine Swynford, whose children had been specifically barred from the succession; his father, Edmund, Earl of Richmond, was the bastard son of Catherine of Valois, widow of Edward VI, by one of her courtiers, Owen Tudor.

Henry silenced his opponents – and ended the War of the Roses – by marrying Elizabeth of York, Edward IV's eldest daughter. At one stroke he unified their houses and allowed England to begin an unprecedented period of internal peace, economic growth and social change.

In 1487 John de la Pole (Edward's nephew) landed with 2,000 troops in support of Lambert Simnel, who tried to pass himself off as the real Earl of Warwick. De la Pole was killed at the Battle of Stoke and Simnel given a job in the royal kitchens! Ten years later a Flemish boy, Perkin Warbeck, found support in Irish and European Yorkist circles for his claim to be Richard, youngest of the princes murdered in the Tower of London. Warbeck was lodged in the Tower and hanged in 1499 when he tried to escape.

Henry VII's greatest achievements were to re-establish the financial well-being of the crown and re-assert the authority of royal law. He even saw to it that conflict could be profitable. In 1489 the French threatened to seize the Duchy of Brittany. Instead of declaring war, Henry negotiated a treaty in which he disclaimed all historic rights to French territory except Calais and received £159,000 in return.

In 1501 he arranged the marriage of his elder son, Arthur, to the Spanish princess Catherine of Aragon, and in 1503 that of his daughter, Margaret, to Scotland's King James IV. Arthur was to die only a year after his marriage, leaving the way clear for his brother Henry to become sovereign of a nation that his father left in fine fettle when he died in 1509.

Henry VIII

Henry VIII inherited something rare in early English history – a secure throne, a solvent treasury and a reasonably united, prosperous kingdom. Only one important aspect of the bad old days remained – the all-powerful Roman Catholic Church. It would be he who destroyed this last vestige of medievalism.

Aged 18 when he inherited the throne, Henry was content at first to enjoy the benefits of kingship – making England one of the centers of Renaissance art and learning in the process – and leave the ruling to Thomas Wolsey, his chancellor. The son of an Ipswich butcher, Wolsey was made Archbishop of York in 1514, Lord Chancellor and cardinal legate a year later, and a papal legate in 1524. Together, king and cardinal pitched England into international politics and occasional war, learning quickly that England no longer ranked as a European superpower.

The major player was now Emperor Charles V, conqueror of Italy and a man who now treated the Pope like a court chaplain. His Italian victory in

1525 coincided disastrously with Henry VIII's decision to get rid of his wife, the 42-year-old Catherine of Aragon, and marry his lover, Anne Boleyn. He had married the much older Catherine when his brother, Arthur, died and his father persisted in retaining a liaison with Spain. Unfortunately, Catherine was also Charles V's aunt and he was happy to block Henry's divorce petition to the Pope for three years. When a Vatican court finally ruled against Henry in 1529, Wolsey was blamed and dismissed from all his offices. He died just before his trial for treason was due to start.

Determined to have his way, Henry moved towards a break with Rome. In truth, the old church was riddled with corruption, a ready target for reformers like the German monk, Martin Luther, and object of derision in England by those who still followed John Wycliffe's teachings. With Wolsey and his papal authority gone, Henry ordered the so-called Reformation Parliament to establish his superiority over Rome in England. During the course of its seven-year sitting Parliament stripped the Pope of all legal and financial jurisdiction.

In January 1533 Henry married the now pregnant Anne Boleyn in secret. He only had eight months to rid himself of Catherine, escape charges of bigamy and ensure Anne's child was born in wedlock. Thomas Cranmer, Wolsey's successor as archbishop, aided Henry by declaring the king's first marriage null and void. Anne was crowned queen and three months later gave birth to a daughter. Henry was stunned. He already had a daughter, Mary, by Catherine and wanted a son to carry on the Tudor line.

Destruction of the Monasteries

✤

The break with Rome became final in 1534 when the Act of Supremacy proclaimed that Henry was supreme head of the church in England. He moved against Rome's English properties, ordered the monasteries to be destroyed and seized their lands. These he sold off to swell the crown's coffers. Those who balked at Henry's assumption of religious supremacy – including Thomas More, Wolsey's successor as Lord Chancellor, and Bishop John Fisher – were executed. Henry had to crush a number of rebellions and execute their leaders.

Anne Boleyn's inability to produce further children led to her execution for infidelity in 1536. Eleven days after Anne's execution Henry married Jane Seymour, and 16 months later the future Edward VI was born. No matter that Jane died as a consequence – Henry had a legitimate male heir.

Henry married three times more. The first (Anne of Cleves) was to cement his relationship with the Lutheran princes of Germany, the second (Katharine

Howard) was for love, and the third (Katharine Parr) was to give himself a nursemaid in his declining years. Anne of Cleves was dropped when the political climate changed in Europe, while Katharine Howard was executed when Henry learned she'd had affairs before and during their marriage. Katharine Parr outlived the king, married the admiral of England, Thomas, Lord Seymour of Sudeley, but died in 1548 giving birth to a daughter.

Henry himself died in 1547, leaving the nine-year-old Edward VI with the impossible task of following in a giant's footsteps.

The Battle of Flodden

✤

Henry VIII was faced with only one major military challenge at home during his reign. That came from Scotland and his brother-in-law, King James IV, in 1513.

To honor his recently made alliance with France and divert English troops from the Pas de Calais area, James crossed the English border with some 30,000 men and artillery in August. Thomas, Earl of Surrey – Henry's lieutenant in the north – raised a 20,000-strong force to meet James, requesting that he wait until September 9 to engage in battle.

Unbelievably, James agreed. The two armies met at Flodden, near Branxton, Northumberland and despite superior Scottish manpower, Surrey was victorious. Among the 10,000 Scottish dead were King James and many of his highest officers of church and state.

Sir Thomas More

✦

A talented and gifted polymath – he was a lawyer, diplomat, author and poet – Thomas More was also, fatally, a man of principle. When he refused to acknowledge Anne Boleyn's legitimacy as queen and Henry VIII's position as head of the English church, his brilliant career was ended by the executioner's axe. He would be recognized as a saint of the Catholic Church in 1935, along with a number of other English martyrs.

Born in London in 1477, the son of a lawyer, More studied at the University of Oxford and was a barrister before becoming a priest. In 1516 he published *Utopia* (literally, "Nowhere"), an allegorical account of an ideal society in which a form of communism is the only defense against selfish egoism in public and private life. Two years later More completed his *History of King Richard III*, the first masterpiece of historical biography and later inspiration for Shakespeare's play about the tyrant.

Appointed to the king's council in 1518, More was

knighted two years later. He publicly attacked the heresies of Martin Luther and in 1529 became Henry VIII's chancellor, despite his open support for the Catholic Church. In 1534 his refusal to swear an oath of loyalty to Anne Boleyn – which included a repudiation of papal supremacy – led to his arrest, trial and beheading in 1535.

The Mary Rose

✤

During a review of his naval fleet in Portsmouth on July 19, 1545, Henry VIII and his courtiers were appalled when the *Mary Rose* – pride of the fleet – mysteriously rolled over and sank in a matter of minutes. Almost 600 men died in the disaster.

The *Mary Rose* lay in the Portsmouth mud until the 1970s when marine archaeologists managed to lift her remarkably intact shell to the surface and sift through the thousands of artifacts the wreck contained – from longbows and arrows, musical instruments and backgammon sets to pewter dishes used by ships' officers. It was, in brief, a superb time capsule for historians to explore.

The human skeletons found were given Christian burials and the wreck itself housed in a huge museum which remains a leading tourist attraction and education center.

Peasants are Revolting!

❧

Edward may have been the son Henry VIII wanted but he was a sickly child destined to live only six years as king. Real power passed to his brother-in-law, Edward Seymour, Earl of Hertford. He became Duke of Somerset and Lord Protector shortly after Edward's reign began, but proved more idealistic than practical.

One of his first moves was to repeal or modify Henry VIII's draconian treason and heresy laws. This only created an outbreak of religious and social fury as long-silenced tongues were freed. Seymour tried to still these by introducing the Prayer Book of 1549. The work of Thomas Cranmer, it sought to unify the various Protestant beliefs but only antagonized Protestants and Catholics alike.

Seymour's protectorship also saw rampant inflation, a false boom in wool prices and an increase in land enclosures. Disgruntled peasants in Cornwall and Devon rose up against the Prayer Book in 1549, their cause aided by a revolt in Norfolk. Seymour embroiled

England in confrontation with Scotland (which soon included France) that ended in defeat. Arrested and stripped of office, he was executed two years later.

He was replaced by John Dudley, Earl of Warwick, who became Duke of Northumberland. A man of action, Dudley pulled out of Scotland, returned Boulogne (which Henry VIII had taken) to France, imprisoned many conservative bishops and allied himself to the most extreme elements of Protestantism. Civil order was restored with ruthless efficiency, priests were turned into government appointees, a new Prayer Book was unconditionally Protestant.

When it became clear that young King Edward was dying of consumption, Dudley tried to stop the succession of Mary – daughter of Henry VIII and Catherine of Aragon – who was a Roman Catholic. Dudley had Mary declared illegitimate and nominated the 15-year-old Lady Jane Grey, granddaughter of Henry VIII's sister, the Duchess of Suffolk, and (coincidentally) his own daughter-in-law. When Edward died on July 6, 1553 the people rallied to Mary. Catholic or not, she was a true Tudor. Nine days later Dudley, Lady Jane and Lord Suffolk were consigned to the Tower of London, where Jane and her father were beheaded.

𝔅loody 𝔐ary

❖

𝔄lso known as "Bloody Mary" for good reason, Mary I's five-year reign was marked by a final three years of barbarous bloodletting, involvement in a war which saw the loss of Calais, England's last European outpost, and her death at the relatively young age of 42, a broken woman.

A devout Catholic, Mary dreamed of returning England to the old faith. It was also, she felt, her duty to marry Philip of Spain, her Hapsburg cousin and the son of Charles V, the man who had defended her mother, Catherine of Aragon. She married him in 1554 and, shortly after – having promised the owners of former monastic properties that they could retain them – had Parliament repeal Henry VIII's Act of Supremacy and petition for reunion with Rome.

Both enterprises proved fruitless. Her marriage was loveless and childless and she faced an immediate civil revolt against a return to Catholicism. Believing that dissenters would respond to a show of force,

Mary began an orgy of execution by public burning at London's Smithfield Market. The first of an eventual 300 men and women martyred this way during the next three years included Protestant leaders Cranmer, Ridley, Latimer and Hooper.

When her husband's Hapsburg cousins declared war on France, England was disastrously dragged into the conflict. When Mary died in November 1558 her relieved subjects celebrated the succession of her sister, Elizabeth, with ringing bells and – ironically – bonfires.

Good Queen Bess

✤

The challenge facing the 25-year-old Elizabeth I in 1558 was to settle the social discord, political floundering and international humiliation of the past decade. The fact that she achieved this and went on to enjoy an extraordinary 45-year reign is testament to her personal strength of will and political skills.

Settlement of religious division was largely achieved by amending her title to "supreme governor" (not "head") of the church, changing the Prayer Book to make it more acceptable to Catholics and reviving some of the old papal trappings of church ceremonies. Catholics proved better losers than uncompromising Protestant radicals, the future Puritans, who were soon in dispute with their new queen.

Determined to be queen in fact as well as name, Elizabeth tamed the House of Commons with a mixture of tact and firmness, appointing a council of able trustworthy men to help her. These included William Cecil, her principal secretary and lord treasurer, and Matthew Parker, Archbishop of Canterbury.

She did not forget the ordinary folk. In 1601 her Poor Law assured a minimum standard of living for a nation suffering widespread poverty, unemployment and vagrancy. Parishes were charged with providing work for the able-bodied, charity for the aged, sick and disabled, and punishing the idle. It was a revolutionary concept.

Revolutions of other kinds were also taking place under Elizabeth I. By 1640 almost all gentry and merchants were literate and the years between 1560 and 1650 saw an explosion of school-building and educational endowment. That, in turn, created the cultural revolution that produced Shakespeare, Marlowe, Sir Francis Bacon and John Donne, among others.

As poets and playwrights put their dreams on paper, Elizabethan adventurers headed for the open sea. New trade routes were opened with Russia and in 1562 England began sailing to Africa in search of slaves for West Indian planatations. Sir Francis Drake circumnavigated the globe between 1577 and 1580 – plundering a great deal of Spanish gold in the process – while Sir Walter Raleigh established the ill-fated "lost colony" of Roanoke, North Carolina. The East India Company was founded to organize trading with the Orient.

Elizabeth's Spanish War

❧

It was only a matter of time before rivalry with Spain led to war. When Mary, Queen of Scots was executed in 1587, Philip II of Spain was Europe's strongest leader, his empire extending into France and the Netherlands. Drake's looting of Spanish ships on his voyage was clearly piracy, as was the refusal of English captains to recognize Spain's claims to trade monopolies wherever its national flag flew.

The failure of the Spanish Armada in 1587 did not end Elizabeth's Spanish war, but it marked the point at which Spain began protecting what it had rather than expanding its empire further. The cost of two decades of war forced Elizabeth to sell almost a quarter of all crown lands and rely on parliamentary allowances from a Commons demanding ever-greater powers in return. Even worse, perhaps, was the rise of Puritanism.

This reached crisis point in 1586 when Puritans called for legislation in the House of Commons to abolish bishops and the Anglican Prayer Book.

Elizabeth realized that her realm now included idealists who claimed spiritual authority from – and owed a greater allegiance to – a higher power than the crown.

The final years of Elizabth's life were difficult. As her popularity waned, she also faced the only palace revolution of her reign when her long-time favorite, the Earl of Essex, disobeyed her order to remain in Ireland on a military expedition. His life ended on the scaffold in 1601. When Elizabeth died on March 24, 1603, there was a palpable sense of relief as men anticipated a new century, a new dynasty and the prospect of a man – and not a woman – on the throne of a united England and Scotland.

Mary, Queen of Scots

❦

A prisoner in England since 1568 when she'd been forced to abdicate her Scottish throne in favor of her infant son, James VI — Mary of Scotland posed a substantial threat to her English cousin, Elizabeth I. To many, the fact that Mary was Henry VIII's grand-niece and a Catholic meant that she, not Elizabeth, was the rightful successor to "Bloody Mary."

As religious turmoil mounted Elizabeth came under constant pressure to rid herself of the threat posed by Mary and her followers. She refused to do so for almost 19 years, only acting when Mary played into the hands of her political and religious enemies by involving herself in a number of schemes to unseat the queen.

Mary's final fatal mistake was to be part of the so-called Babington Plot of 1586. Hatched by Anthony Babington, member of a secret society which aided Jesuit missionaries, this went awry when correpon-dence between him and Mary was intercepted.

Mary's complicity in an assassination plot was

enough to have her tried and executed for high treason. In February 1587 she was beheaded at Fotheringhay Castle, near Northampton. It was her son James who would rule England, but only when Elizabeth I herself died.

John Knox

✦

Principal leader of the Scottish Reformation, John Knox was born around 1514 near Haddington, Lothian. Inspired by George Wishart, a reforming preacher burned for heresy in 1546, Knox began his own work in the ancient cathedral city of St Andrews a year later.

After French forces captured St Andrews, Knox was one of a number of Protestants captured and carried off to serve as slaves in French galleys. His health was irreperably damaged by the time English intervention secured their release 19 months later. Given charge of preaching the Protestant faith in Berwick-upon-Tweed and Newcastle during Edward VI's reign, Knox had become a preacher in and around the southern counties of Kent and Buckinghamshire by the time of the Catholic Mary Tudor's accession in 1553.

Fleeing to Frankfurt am Main, Germany, Knox became minister to a mainly Puritan congregation before moving to minister to a growing number of

English exiles in Geneva. He returned to Scotland in 1559, finding himself pitched into a church vs state battle, with occupying French forces loyal to Mary, Queen of Scots, harrying him and other Scottish civic and religious leaders.

In 1560, 10,000 English troops joined the Scottish Protestants in ejecting the French. Knox was now free to preach and play his part in creating the Church of Scotland. He suffered a stroke before preaching a final sermon in St Giles' Cathedral, Edinburgh, in 1572.

The Spanish Armada

❧

Spain's decision to launch an attack on England in 1587 followed years of English interference in Spanish-held Holland. In 1585, following the assassination of the Protestant leader William of Orange, Elizabeth despatched an English army of 6,000 under the command of the Earl of Leicester. Philip II decided to act.

He began to assemble a fleet of 130 galleons which would create a naval blockade in the Channel long enough for the Duke of Parma's army – based at Dunkirk – to invade southern England. In April 1587 Elizabeth sent Drake to Spain where he launched a strike at the part of the Spanish fleet based in Cádiz. It succeeded only in postponing the inevitable.

Philip's Armada would prove invincible in name only. Technically and numerically outclassed by an English fleet of 200 newly built and fully prepared ships, the Armada also ran into Britain's most effective traditional line of defense – foul weather.

Buffeted by gales, the Armada was decimated as it tried to escape home by sailing around Scotland and Ireland. Only 85 galleons reached Spain. Ten had been captured, sunk or driven aground by English guns and 25 were lost to wind and stormy seas. Another 12 simply disappeared, their fate unknown.

William Shakespeare

❧

Brightest jewel in the Elizabethan artistic crown, William Shakespeare's contribution to world literature remains unsurpassed, both as playwright and poet. Author of dozens of comedies, tragedies and historical sagas – many of which dramatized the lives of English monarchs – he also wrote peerless verse, either as long narrative poems or in the form of sonnets.

Born in Stratford-upon-Avon in 1564, he was the eldest son of a glover and wool dealer. He probably gained his education at Stratford Grammar School where Greek and Latin poetry and philosophy were studied. At the age of 18 he married Anne Hathaway, a farmer's daughter eight years older than him and already pregnant. Their daughter, Susanna, was born less than six months later. In 1585 Anne gave birth to twins – a son, Hamnet, who would die aged 11, and his second daughter, Judith.

Shortly after, Shakespeare left to make his fortune in London. He was an almost immediate success as a writer – less so as the actor he wanted to be – and in

1594 was invited by theater manager Richard Burbage to join his Lord Chamberlain's Men company as a partner. That winter Queen Elizabeth invited them to entertain her at court. They would play an average of three command performances a year in the future.

The stream of plays which poured from Shakespeare's pen during the next five years also captured the public's acclaim. Now wealthy, Shakespeare bought New Place, a large mansion in Stratford, for his wife and daughters, though he continued to live in London. The accession of James I in 1603 provided Shakespeare with a new and equally devoted royal patron. The merging of Burbage's company with the rival King's Men also gave him two theaters – The Globe and Blackfriars – for which to write new works.

Gradually withdrawing from public life, by 1612 he had retired to Stratford. It was there that he died four years later, and where he was buried – in the church where he'd been baptized 52 years earlier. A few months later friends arranged for his collected plays to be published in one volume and the full glory of Shakespeare's talent was saved for posterity.

Christopher Marlowe

❧

Shakespeare's most important predecessor in English drama and most noted for his dramatic blank verse, "Kit" Marlowe was also a hellraiser, probably a government spy and died – stabbed to death in a Deptford lodging house – during an argument over a bill, aged only 29.

Born in 1564, in Canterbury, Marlowe was the second child and eldest son of a local shoemaker and entered the King's School 13 years later. A year after that he began desultory studies at Corpus Christi College, Cambridge. He was only granted his master's degree in 1587 when a Privy Council letter explained his many absences from Cambridge as his being employed "on matters touching the benefit of his country."

Establishing himself in London as a formidable talent, Marlowe's six-year career was marked by constant brushes with the law as much as his plays – which included the two-part *Tamburlaine the Great*, *Dido, Queen of Carthage*, *Faustus* and *The Jew of Malta*

– and his poetry. The greatest of his poetic works, *Hero and Leander*, remained unfinished when he died.

It remains a mystery whether Marlowe's death was a contracted murder or a tragic end to a drunken brawl. Whatever the truth, it robbed England – and the world – of a formidably talented man whose few surviving works promised so much more.

Sir Francis Drake

✦

The most famous seaman of the Elizabethan Age, Drake was born in the early 1540s, in Devon, the son of a poor tenant farmer and ardent Protestant lay preacher. Poverty and a Catholic uprising drove Drake's family to Kent in 1549, where they found lodgings in an abandoned naval hulk near Chatham. Apprenticed to a small coastal vessel, Drake mastered the art of sailing in some of the world's wildest seas before enlisting in the fleet owned by the wealthy Hawkins family of Plymouth, Devon – distant relations of his father.

During his second voyage to the West Indies – in the company of John Hawkins – Drake and his companions were ambushed by a Spanish fleet at San Juan de Ulúa, off the Mexican coast. Only Drake and Hawkins managed to evade capture. Queen Elizabeth encouraged his dreams of revenge against Spain and sanctioned the piratical raids he carried out during the next few years.

In 1577 Elizabeth backed Drake as leader of an

expedition to pass around South America through the Strait of Magellan and explore the coast beyond. Leading a fleet of five small ships from his own *Golden Hind*, Drake's three-year voyage would see him circumnavigate the globe and establish trade with numerous new-found territories, including the west coast of Canada. He also returned with Spanish booty and foreign spices.

Appointed mayor of Plymouth in 1581, Drake established a civic water supply that served the city for 300 years. He had his enemies, but Elizabeth I was not one of them. In 1585 she gave him command of a fleet of 25 ships to harass Spain. He was astoundingly successful, capturing Santiago in the Cape Verde Islands, and plundering cities in Colombia, Florida and San Domingo. Spain's international credit almost foundered as a result.

Although he was second in command of the English fleet which confronted the Armada in 1588 (Lord Howard was admiral), it was Drake who prompted the use of fire ships to drive Spanish galleons out of Calais and into the gales which raged through the Channel. Undisputed hero of the day, Drake achieved a popularity unequaled by any until Horatio Nelson emerged more than 200 years later.

The newly ennobled Sir Francis died in 1596, once more in the West Indies to attack his old foe. His fleet hit by fever, Drake himself succumbed and was buried at sea off the town of Portobello, Panama.

5

The Stuarts
1603–1714

❖

James I

❖

Elizabeth I's decision to remain unmarried and childless opened the way for James VI of Scotland, a member of the Stuart family, to become king of England. Retitling himself James I this accomplished and learned monarch joined his two nations peacefully, laying the foundations for what would become the United Kingdom. There would, inevitably, be some on both sides who refused to bury the hatchet.

A philosopher prince, James wrote political treatises, could debate theology with prelates and was an avid student of statecraft. He also commissioned a new English Bible (now known as the King James Version). James cleverly began his reign with a progress through the realm, awarding knighthoods to those whose hospitality he enjoyed. Less happily, he also received a petition signed by a thousand clergymen asking him to address the unfinished business of church reform and inherited a royal budget deficit of £400,000.

It was James's intention to create a church capable of including all moderate Protestants and Catholics. This would founder in the chaos of the 1605 Gunpowder Plot, which led to inevitable reprisals against Catholics and block his way to exhibiting leniency toward them in later years. The royal budget would prove no easier to solve and by 1624 – the year before his death – James's debt had risen to £1 million.

As ever, court politics were dominated by family factions. James appointed a number of members of the Howard family to senior posts. They formed the core of a pro-Spanish clique which also wanted better treatment of English Catholics. Their opposition came from a faction headed by Queen Anne, the Archbishop of Canterbury and the Duke of

Buckingham, James's lover. They wanted an aggressive Protestant domestic and foreign policy.

Only to a point, however. In 1623 the ever-pragmatic Buckingham traveled secretly with Prince Charles to Madrid, intending to arrange the marriage of James's heir to the Spanish king's daughter. They returned home rejected, humiliated and determined to get King James to declare war on Spain. The ailing sovereign did so, thus confirming his kingdom's involvement in the pan-European Thirty Years War. When he died, in March 1625, James I left a kingdom firmly controlled by Buckingham and Charles I.

The Gunpowder Plot

❧

In the spring of 1605 a group of English Catholics – Robert Catesby, Guy Fawkes, Thomas Winter, John Wright and Thomas Percy – hatched a conspiracy to blow up Parliament when King James and his eldest son, Henry, were present. They hoped that the ensuing confusion would give Catholics the chance to seize power.

Renting a cellar which extended under the Palace of Westminster, they stored 20 barrels of gunpowder which Guy Fawkes supplied and set their date with destiny as November 5.

During the summer the conspirators recruited others and it was one of these, Francis Tresham, who advised his brother-in-law, Lord Monteagle, that he should miss Parliament on that day. Monteagle raised the alarm and Guy Fawkes was captured in the cellar on November 4. He revealed the names of his co-conspirators under torture. Catesby, Percy and two others were killed while resisting arrest. The others were tried for treason, found guilty and executed in January 1606.

In that same month Parliament established November 5 as a day of public thanksgiving. What has become known as Guy Fawkes Night is still celebrated with bonfires topped by effigies of the treacherous conspirator, and firework displays.

Titles for Sale

❧

One of James I's least reputable devices for reducing his ever-increasing debts was the sale of titles. Although it had long been common practice for monarchs to reward their favorites with new or grander titles, no one before had blatantly offered the power and prestige of earldoms and dukedoms to those with nothing to recommend them except an ability to raise the asking price.

During James's reign hundreds of new earls and dukes were created this way. Their descendants were entitled to take their place in the House of Lords – Britain's upper legislative chamber – and vote on crucial matters of state, even rejecting legislation already passed by the democratically elected House of Commons.

In 1997 the government of Prime Minister Tony Blair announced its intention of excluding heriditary peers from the Lords and creating a new, more democratic upper chamber of Parliament.

Charles I

As different to his father as could be, Charles I was shy, tiny and had a speech defect that made public speaking an ordeal. He had not been raised to rule but had that duty thrust on him when his brother, Henry, died suddenly in 1612. Although he had the support of his queen, Henrietta Maria, and Lord Buckingham, Charles was compromised by the fact that Henrietta was not only French but also Roman Catholic. Buckingham's assassination in 1628 would lose him an adviser whose absence would prove crucial.

Fatally committed to an expensive and pointless war with Spain – and briefly with France – Charles clashed with Parliament over funding. Defeats for Buckingham's forces led to his murder and a void in Charles's military and domestic policies, the most contentious of which was religion. His bid to tread a middle path outraged extremists in Protestant, Calvinist and Catholic churches in England, Scotland and Ireland. By 1640 Scottish troops invaded England and captured Newcastle and the English forces were sent to quell rebellion in Ireland.

Parliament stepped in to wrest control of the army from the king in 1642 and the kingdom was pitched into a three-year civil war which saw royalist forces pitched against Parliament's newly formed New Model Army. Despite early victories, Charles's forces were eventually defeated and he was forced to accede to Parliament's demands.

Discontent with pay arrears led to a mutiny in Parliament's army a year later and a second civil war, the climax of which saw the New Model Army regiments of Oliver Cromwell defeat Charles's Scottish allies at Preston. In December 1648 politicized New Model soldiers arrested 45 members of parliament still advocating settlement with Charles and barred 186 more from attending. Charles, too, was arrested and tried by a court of parliamentarians, civilians and army officers. Found guilty, he was beheaded outside his own palace on January 30, 1649. One witness recorded in his diary that "such a groan went up as I had never before heard," as the executioner's axe fell.

The Pilgrim Fathers

❖

The first permanent colony in New England was founded in 1620 by a group of 102 intrepid adventurers who left the English port of Plymouth aboard the *Mayflower*. Thirty-five of these were members of the English Separatist Church, a radical Puritan faction, who had earlier fled England for Holland to escape persecution.

Seeking religious freedom and a more abundant life, they were financed by a London stock company. The non-Separatists on the *Mayflower* were hired by that company to protect its interests. The phrase "Pilgrim Fathers" did not come into common usage until 1820, when the orator Daniel Webster first coined it.

Oliver Cromwell: The Early Years

❧

Lord Protector of the republican Commonwealth of England, Scotland and Ireland between 1653 and 1658, Oliver Cromwell was a devout Calvinist whose convictions led to the enforcement of a Puritan regime which oversaw the persecution of liberal Protestants, the desecration of churches considered too "papist" in their decorations, the systematic massacre of thousands of Irish Catholic dissenters Cromwell dismissed as primitive, savage and superstitious, and the closure of most places of public entertainment considered "sinful."

Born in Huntingdon, Cambridgeshire in 1599, Cromwell was the only son of a former member of parliament and justice of the peace, was educated at the local grammar school and at the age of 21 married the daughter of a titled London merchant who would bear him five sons and four daughters. Elected to Parliament for a second time in 1640, Cromwell was a member of a gentry openly chafing at King Charles's punative taxes and, in his case, corruption in the Church of England.

Cromwell was a gifted and courageous fighting man, initially in his native East Anglia but later in the north. By the end of the first conflict in 1645 he had risen to become deputy commander of the New Model Army. At first keen that Parliament should settle its differences with Charles, Cromwell was outraged when the king made a treaty with Scottish rebels. Though he was not in London when Charles was arrested, it was Cromwell who signed the king's death warrant at his trial.

Oliver Cromwell: Lord Protector

❖

During the first three years following Charles I's execution Cromwell remained a soldier in action against royalists in Ireland and Scotland. His Irish campaign was brutal and climaxed in the massacre of a rebel garrison at Drogheda. In 1650 he succeeded Sir Thomas Fairfax as army commander and led troops against Scottish supporters of the future king, Charles II. A year later he crushed the young king's army at Worcester.

When a nationwide army mutiny against Parliament in 1653 could not be solved by mediation, Cromwell ordered the House closed and called a new Parliament of nominated members. This so-called "Assembly of Saints" proved too radical for Cromwell and he assumed the title Lord Protector – a de facto dictator to whom a council of state reported.

His first act before summoning his first Parliament in September 1654 was to pass more than 80 ordinances to reform the law, establish a Puritan Church and permit religious toleration outside it, and to promote education and decentralize administration. His own religious tolerance did not extend as far as troublesome Quakers, a number of whose leaders he imprisoned. He did allow Jews to return to England, fostered the cause of grammar schools and founded a college in Durham.

Cromwell also ended a war with Holland, formed an alliance with France and seized Spanish West Indies territories – including Jamaica. At home he found the two Parliaments he called no easier to handle than his regal predecessors had and controversially dissolved them both.

The ill health which had plagued him since his Irish campaign took hold in August 1658. Cromwell contracted malaria and died in Whitehall on September 3. His body was secretly interred in Westminster Abbey 13 days before his state funeral on November 23. In 1661, after the restoration of King Charles II to the throne, Cromwell's remains were taken from his tomb and hung at Tyburn, where criminals were executed, before being reburied under the gallows. His head was impaled on a pole at Westminster Hall, where it remained until the end of Charles II's reign.

Richard Cromwell

❧

If Oliver Cromwell had wanted to prove his belief that hereditary inheritance is a deeply flawed concept, he could have done no better than nominate his own son, Richard, as his successor. He did, and Richard's nine-month tenure of supreme office was a disaster.

Aged 32 when he became Lord Protector in September 1658, Richard Cromwell immediately offended high-ranking officers by taking charge of the army, a task for which he had no experience or aptitude. When conflict between Parliament and the army led the army to establish a strategy council, Parliament forbade it to meet without Richard's permission.

The officers responded by recalling the Parliament Oliver Cromwell had dissolved three years earlier. This assembly dismissed Richard and he fled to Paris to avoid the creditors of huge debts he'd amassed. Living there under the alias John Clarke he later moved to Geneva, not returning to England until 1680. He lived in seclusion until his death in 1712.

The Merry Monarch

✦

Britain's flirtation with republicanism ended not with a bang but with a whimpered request to the exiled Charles II to come home and end a state of near-anarchy by taking his place on the throne. This request – from General George Monck, one of Oliver Cromwell's lieutenants – was made knowing that most of the population would welcome the restoration of a monarchy. Charles issued a declaration promising a general amnesty, equitable settlements of land disputes and payment of all army back-pay. He was welcomed back to England on May 25, 1660, reaching London on his 30th birthday.

Charles II's 25-year rule ("the Restoration period") was marked by his ability to adapt to political change and so steer his country through the continued scuffles that broke out between Anglicans, Catholics, Presbyterians and Puritans. His foreign policy saw him acquire possession of Tangier and Bombay through marriage to the Portuguese Princess Catherine of Braganza in 1661, a new alliance with

France against the Netherlands, and the capture of New York from the Dutch in 1664. In the process Charles oversaw the modernization of the British fleet.

With the dourness of Puritanism lifted, the country witnessed a reflowering of artistic enterprise. The Fire of London in 1666 not only helped eradicate the Great Plague but enabled the architect Christopher Wren to reshape the heart of the capital.

Popularly known as "the Merry Monarch," Charles was notorious for his active love life. He is known to have fathered at least 18 illegitimate children, many of whom were rewarded with titles and land. The greatest love of his life seems to have been Nell Gwynn, an actress and former orange seller. Queen Catherine, sadly, proved unable to carry a baby full-term. This created fears that Charles's brother, James – the Catholic Duke of York – would provide the heir to the throne.

This unthinkable prospect led to the most serious political storm of Charles II's reign. It came in 1678 via Titus Oates, a former Anglican cleric who claimed to have evidence that Catholics planned to murder the king to ensure James's succession. Charles was forced to send his brother into exile and deny the legitimacy of his own heir, the Duke of Monmouth.

The people's trust – and his popularity – restored, Charles's last years were marked by civil stability, a healthy treasury and an efficient administration. When he died, in 1685, the country was enjoying the kind of tranquil prosperity Charles had always wanted.

Samuel Pepys

❖

A remarkable character who rose from humble beginnings to work at senior level for Charles II, Samuel Pepys was an inveterate diarist. It is thanks to his journals, which were first published in 1825, that we have a complete and absorbing picture of life in Restoration London between 1660 and 1669.

Born in London in 1633, Pepys (pronounced "peeps") was a tailor's son. By the time of his death in 1703, Pepys had variously served as a member of parliament, been president of the Royal Society, master of Trinity House and the Clothworkers' Company and a baron of the Cinque Ports. He was also the earliest secretary of the Admiralty, a confidant of King Charles II and James II and friend of some of the country's greatest creative minds, including the architect Sir Christopher Wren, scientist Sir Isaac Newton and poet John Dryden.

His unyielding demands for efficiency and honesty made Pepys formidable enemies. Greatest of these was Lord Shaftesbury who, in 1678, unjustly accused

Pepys of complicity in the murder of a London magistrate. When Pepys provided a solid alibi, Shaftesbury produced a blackmailer, John Scott, who leveled charges of treason good enough to have Pepys confined to the Tower of London. Able to assemble damning evidence against his accuser, Pepys was released and returned to King Charles's service in 1684. Charles gave him responsibility for rebuilding the navy and controlling the largest budget ever granted a department of state.

The Great Plague

✤

More than 75,000 Londoners are believed to have died in the plague epidemic which ravaged the capital from late 1664 to early 1666. It was not an isolated event – 40,000 are known to have perished in a similar outbreak 30 years earlier. This latest one was severe enough to drive Charles II and his court out of London for eight months.

The first symptoms of plague were flushed rosy cheeks and cold-like sneezing. So bad was the smell of disease and decay that people took to holding nosegays – small bunches of flowers – to "protect" themselves. These two aspects were immortalized in the nursery rhyme:

> Ring a ring o' roses
> A pocket full of posies
> A-tishoo, a-tishoo
> All fall down.

Although the Great Fire of London is credited with ending the plague, modern opinion is that it was pure coincidence, because the plague also subsided in other cities around the same time.

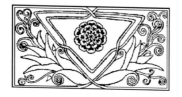

The Fire of London

✦

The worst fire in London's history, this conflagration destroyed a large part of the city, including most civic buildings, St Paul's Cathedral, 87 churches and some 13,000 houses between September 2 and 5, 1666.

It began accidentally in the house of a baker in Pudding Lane, near London Bridge. Fanned by a strong wind, the fire spread through the warren of timbered buildings. Just when it looked as if it had been defeated, flames broke out anew at the Temple and gunpowder was used to blow up houses to create a firebreak. At the height of the destruction the River Thames was packed with vessels carrying people and their salvaged possessions to safety.

Although plans to completely redesign the city were presented to Charles II, he decided to retain the age-old maze of streets and alleys, giving the task of rebuilding them to Robert Hooke. Sir Christopher Wren was charged with creating a new St Paul's Cathedral and 53 churches.

James II

❧

The three-year reign of Charles II's Catholic brother was always going to be tough going, and the new king did little to help calm the fears of the Protestant factions by proving himself stern, uncompromising and despotic. One of his first acts was to order the execution of the Duke of Monmouth, his nephew and rival to the throne.

James's pro-Catholic policies became too much when his second wife, Mary – also a Catholic – gave birth to a son, duly named James. Although James had two daughters by his marriage to Anne Hyde, a Protestant who raised the girls in the same faith, the prospect of another Catholic king drove Protestant leaders to the unconstitutional step of inviting the Dutch prince, William of Orange, and his wife Mary (James II's eldest daughter) to England.

William landed unopposed by English forces and James fled for France, dropping the Great Seal of Office into the Thames – an action deemed tantamount to abdication. William and Mary were declared joint sovereigns, and while James would attempt to regain his crown, his defeat at the Battle of the Boyne ended his dreams. They would be continued by his son, called "the Old Pretender," when his father died in France a year later.

Battle of the Boyne

✦

The end of James II's ambition to reclaim his throne came on July 11, 1690 when the forces of King William III overwhelmed his on the banks of this Irish river.

Having failed to take Enniskillen and Londonderry (the latter famously defended by Protestant apprentices who barred the city's gates to frustrate James's Catholic commanders), James marshaled an army of 21,000 men. These comprised about 7,000 French infantry, some regular Irish cavalry and largely untrained Irish infantry and dragoons. William's force of 35,000 was made up of Dutch Blue Guards, two regiments of French Huguenots and contingents of Danish, Prussian, Finnish and Swiss mercenaries, and some English supporters.

James fled when William's army launched a pincer attack and left the country. Although his Jacobite troops would continue their hopeless war for another year, James's cause was lost. The Battle of the Boyne is still celebrated by Northern Ireland Protestants with triumphant marches every year. The date they use – July 12 – is actually the anniversary of the more decisive Battle of Aughrim, which took place a year after the Boyne.

William and Mary

❖

𝔄 contrasting couple – Mary II was a popular and gentle woman who devoted herself to good works while William III was a stolid Dutchman who relied overmuch on his fellow countrymen for company and advice – England's new joint rulers enjoyed a loving but childless marriage. William's solo reign would last for eight more years after Mary's death from smallpox in 1694.

William signaled his intention to be a strong and ruthless sovereign less than three years into his reign when he ordered the massacre of Scottish clansmen at Glencoe and united with Holland in a war against the French, who had supported James II in Ireland.

The move which gained him greatest popularity, however, was his consent to the 1701 Act of Settlement. Under this legislation the crown was to pass – after Princess Anne, James II's second Protestant daughter – only to the next Protestant heir. Henceforth, no Catholics were allowed to reign over what Anne would make a United Kingdom, and no sovereign could marry a Catholic.

The Glencoe Massacre

❦

Many Scottish clans had remained loyal to James II when William of Orange ascended the throne in 1689 – a situation William could not afford to allow to continue. In 1691 he offered an indemnity to all clan chiefs who would swear an oath of allegiance to him before January 1, 1692. Suspecting that many would refuse, so-called "Letters of fire and sword" were drawn up to authorize severe reprisals against any rebels.

In the event, the chiefs took the oath. All, that is, except Alexander MacDonald of Glencoe. He postponed his submission until December 31, 1691 and was then unable to swear his oath until seven days later – there was no magistrate in nearby Fort William to receive it!

King William signed an order for military reprisals and on February 13, 1692 a force of more than 100 soldiers launched a ferocious attack on the unsuspecting MacDonalds. While many managed to escape the slaughter, the chief and 37 others – including women and children – did not. To this day there is bad blood between MacDonalds and Campbells, for John Campbell, Earl of Breadalbane, was complicit in the massacre of his rivals.

Whigs and Tories

❦

Britain's first political parties began to coalesce into definable named groups during the reign of William and Mary – the Whigs and the Tories. In essence, Whigs were the political descendants of Scottish covenanters (derisively named "whiggamores") who'd opposed the future James II's accession to the throne, while Tories (from the equally insulting Irish word *toraidhe* – cattle-thief, bandit or outlaw) were descended from those who had supported James's claim.

During the next 200 years the Whigs would gradually evolve into the modern Liberal Party, so losing their original name. Many of today's Conservatives still refer to themselves as Tories – a name which their opponents use as an epithet, often with undertones of the word's original meanings!

Union with Scotland

❧

Thirty-seven years old when she ascended the throne in 1702, Queen Anne was neither ambitious nor cultured. But she was a High Church Tory with strict notions of the limit of Parliament's authority. It was this which led to her falling out with her closest friend, Sarah, Duchess of Marlborough, whose husband – hero and victor of the Battle of Blenheim during the War of the Spanish Succession – was an avowed Whig.

Married to the unassuming Prince George of Denmark, an avid horticulturist with no known interest in politics, none of their children survived childhood. Anne was to oversee the 1707 Act of Union which saw the end of a Scottish parliament and the creation of a British legislature in London to which Scottish, Welsh and Irish consituencies would return members of parliament and Scottish peers would be summoned to the House of Lords. And so the United Kingdom of Great Britain and Ireland was created.

Especially concerned with church affairs, in 1704 Anne established Queen Anne's Bounty, an emergency fund for impoverished clergy. The last of the Tudors, she was apparently happy to see the House of Hanover become Britain's new royal family. She would not, however, allow any of its members to live in Britain during her lifetime.

The Battle of Blenheim

✦

International disputes as to how Spanish-held territories in Europe were to be governed began with the death of Charles II, the last Spanish Hapsburg king, in 1700. They flared into the Spanish War of Succession — a conflict which saw England form a Grand Alliance with Holland and the Holy Roman Empire. This alliance soon found itself at war with France and its Bavarian allies when French forces seized key ports and cities in the Spanish Netherlands.

Originally sent to Holland as an envoy to forge the Grand Alliance, John Churchill, the Duke of Marlborough, was soon commanding a force which raced 250 miles from Holland to Bavaria in late July 1704 when a Franco-Bavarian army threatened Hapsburg lands.

Marlborough emerged victorious from a battle at Blenheim which lasted for 11 days and nights from August 2. Both sides sustained enormous casualties, but Marlborough's achievement was to save Vienna, drive the French back across the Rhine and end Bavaria's involvement in the war. The Duke's Oxfordshire palace was duly named for his greatest victory, and it was there that his most famous descendant, Sir Winston Churchill, was born in 1874.

6

The House of Hanover
1714–1837

The arrival of German Hanoverian rulers to the British throne was due entirely to the 1701 Act of Settlement which decreed that a Protestant must follow Queen Anne to the throne. George Louis, Elector of Hanover, gained that honor by being the son of Sophia, Electress of Hanover, who was the daughter of James I's own daughter, Elizabeth. A distant relative, then, but still the first Protestant in line. George spoke no English and addressed his ministers in French.

Raised as a soldier, George I's arrival was greeted with enthusiasm by the Whigs, with animosity and hostility from Tories and Jacobites (who supported the rival claim to the throne of James Edward Stuart, the only surviving son of James II), and with supreme indifference from his new subjects, especially as George preferred to spend his time in Hanover and left the country in the care of a cabinet eventually headed by Sir Robert Walpole. George had been married, but divorced and imprisoned his wife for alleged infidelity.

The single greatest threat to George came in the Scottish Jacobite rebellions in 1715 and 1719. James Stuart's forces were easily defeated and the Old Pretender retired to Rome. In 1720 George's involvement in the speculative Whig-backed South Sea Company – a consortium formed to trade with South America – lost him a fortune when the South Sea bubble burst. When George died, of an apoplectic fit in Hanover, his departure was not greatly mourned in Britain.

The First Jacobite Rebellions

Encouraged by the French king, Louis XIV, to launch an offensive against George I, James Stuart – who titled himself "James III of England and James VIII of Scotland" – staged his first rebellion in 1715, with the support of John Erskine, Earl of Mar. An indecisive commander, Erskine saw his troops overwhelmed by the smaller force of John Campbell, Duke of Argyll. He and James fled to France with many co-conspirators.

Moving his court to Rome and then Madrid, James plotted a fresh rebellion. In 1719 he returned to Scotland once more. This time bad weather drove his force back, making a second defeat at Galashiels something of a formality. James returned to Rome for good, all hopes of a Stuart restoration now focused on his young son, Charles.

George II

❧

The last British ruler to lead his troops in battle, George II and his father openly detested each other and it was only the diplomatic skills of Sir Robert Walpole which negotiated an uneasy peace between them in 1720. When George I rewarded Walpole with high office, Walpole lost the prince's trust. George II would have dismissed Walpole when he became king in 1727 but for the timely intervention of his wife, Queen Caroline, a beautiful and astute woman who appears to have been the brains of the royal family.

Walpole managed to convert many Jacobite Tories to the king's side and ensured a Whig majority in Parliament through liberal use of the grateful monarch's patronage. No prominent politician deserted George during the last Jacobite rebellion in 1745, but a growing enmity between George and his son, Frederick Louis, saw the creation of an anti-Walpole faction which forced the prime minister's resignation in 1742.

With Britain embroiled against the French in the eight-year War of the Austrian Succession, George was keen to display his military training and prowess. In 1743 he personally led British troops to victory at Dettingen, near Stuttgart. The task of driving Charles Stuart ("Bonnie Prince Charlie") out of Scotland two years later was given to the ruthlessly efficient Prince William Augustus, Duke of Cumberland, while it was George's new prime minister, William Pitt, who devised the strategy that gave Britain victory in 1763 to end the Seven Years' War against France.

An avid music lover, it was George's patronage which helped the German-born George Frederick Handel to become the preeminent composer of the day. When George II died in 1760, he was succeeded by his grandson, also named George. His estranged son, Frederick Louis, had died nine years earlier, hit by a tennis ball. Well, it beats an arrow in the eye or a red-hot poker . . . !

The Battle of Culloden

✦

In 1745 Charles Edward Stuart – Bonnie Prince Charlie, the son of James Stuart – was urged by Louis XV of France to claim the British throne by force. The 25-year-old prince duly landed in the Hebrides in July and initially enjoyed better fortune than his father, James, had in 1715 or 1719. After taking Edinburgh in September, Charles advanced as far south as the English city of Derby before being forced back into Scotland by the army of William Augustus, Duke of Cumberland.

On April 16, 1746 Charles and Cumberland met at Culloden, east of Inverness. Weak and starving, the 5,000 Jacobite troops were no match for Cumberland's 9,000 Redcoats and cannons. The ensuing battle lasted only 40 minutes, during which more than 1,000 Highlanders were slaughtered. Cumberland reported only 50 casualties among his own men.

During the following weeks Cumberland's forces hunted down and killed at least 1,000 more of

Charles's followers, employing a remorseless brutality that would earn Cumberland the title "Butcher" in Scotland, but prompt Handel to compose "See the Conquering Hero Comes" to commemorate his victory. In England the flower Sweet William was named for him, though Scots still know the same plant as Stinking Willie.

Charles Stuart fled into hiding for five months before escaping to France and permanent exile in Rome. His defeat at Culloden ended all Stuart pretensions to kingship.

Wolfe takes Quebec

❧

Britain's continued war with France was not confined to the European mainland. French territories in North America (modern-day Canada and Louisiana included) also saw British soldiers in action. The appointment of Major-General James Wolfe – who had fought alongside King George at Dettingen and Cumberland at Culloden – to lead an expedition to Quebec in 1759 would prove decisive.

Highly rated by George II – who is reputed to have replied, when advised that Wolfe was mad, that he wished he'd bite some of his other generals – Wolfe proved his mettle by capturing the supposedly impregnable French fort at Quebec with an amphibious force, so ensuring British rule in a province which would nevertheless remain obdurately French-speaking.

Wolfe's victory came at immense personal cost, however. He was killed during the final offensive, so never lived to enjoy the hero-worship his triumph created back home.

The Farmer Who Lost America

❧

Although his 60-year reign is best remembered for Britain's loss of its American colonies and the birth of the United States, the third King George's real fault lay in his unconditional support for a prime minister who made a number of strategic blunders which forced the colonists' hand and made the Declaration of Independence and the American Revolution inevitable. And while his reign ended in victories over the French, thanks to Admiral Nelson and the Duke of Wellington, George had sunk into a madness from which he would never recover.

Unlike his predecessors, George III based himself in England, not Hanover. He also married well and happily, to Charlotte Sophia of Mecklenburg-Strelitz, to make his personal life a happy one. They both adored the countryside – a fact which led to his subjects affectionately calling him "Farmer George."

The resignation of George's original confidant, the Earl of Bute, in 1770, allowed Lord North to become prime minister. It was he who insisted on applying the punitive tea import duties and an East India Company trade monopoly on American colonists which had been introduced three years earlier. Seven years later Britain had lost its greatest single possession and a new nation was born.

In the year that the United States of America came into being, George gained a prime minister – William Pitt, the Younger – who would steer Britain into calmer waters. The two men did fall out over the matter of Catholic political emancipation when George rejected Pitt's solution of allowing Catholics into Parliament.

George's tragic decline into madness and near blindness, and the rule of his son as Prince Regent, were a tragic end for a man who had always meant well but lacked the strength to govern well. When the time came for Britain to fight Napoleon Bonaparte, all major decisions were being made by politicians and the crown's hold on supreme power had begun to be a thing of the past.

The Boston Tea Party

❧

On the night of December 16, 1773 a group of about 60 men swathed in blankets and wearing Mohawk headdresses marched to Griffin's Wharf, Boston and tipped 342 chests containing tea worth £18,000 into the cold waters of the harbor. They were cheered on by a large crowd of fellow Bostonians who, like them, were determined to strike a blow against Britain's enforcement of a tax on imported tea while giving them no say in how those – or any other – taxes would be spent.

Tea was the only imported commodity which remained taxed after a 1767 Act of Parliament which levied import duties on various products was repealed in 1770, so great was the outcry in America. Worse, in 1773 the Tea Act had granted the troubled East India Company exclusive importation and sales rights, so bypassing independent shippers and merchants.

In New York, Charleston and Philadelphia tea agents resigned or canceled orders and merchants refused consignments. The royal governor of Boston ordered that three East India ships should be allowed to deposit their cargoes, and appropriate duties applied. Parliament's reaction to the Boston Tea Party – shutting the city's sea trade down pending payment for the dumped cargo – served only to unite the colonies and make a final showdown a matter of when, not if.

The American War of Independence

❦

Hostilities between American volunteers and British armed forces had been limited to small skirmishes before the Declaration of Independence of 1776 pitched the 13 colonies into a full-scale war that the British had every reason to believe they would win easily. They should have, for the rebels' 20,000-strong resistance force consisted of volunteer civilian militias and a small Continental Army, while the British Army led by Generals William Howe and Lord Cornwallis boasted 42,000 professional soldiers and the support of 30,000 German mercenaries.

While the British enjoyed early victories over the American commander, General George Washington, the decision of France (in 1778), Spain (in 1779) and Holland (a year after that) to take the rebels' side began to tip the balance. A series of victories by Washington pushed the British into an enclave around New York in the north while French ships and land forces laid seige to British-held Savannah in the south.

Cornwallis fought a number of brilliant battles before establishing his base in Yorktown, Virginia. Trapped in a seige laid by the French Count de Rochambeau, Cornwallis surrendered his garrison of 7,000 men on October 19, 1781.

The land war over, American privateers began harassing British vessels, their success at capturing some 1,500 British merchant ships and 12,000 sailors due in no small part to the fact that the French and Dutch navies were able to keep the bulk of British naval forces locked in a struggle to defend the waters around the British Isles.

Britain recognized the independence of the United States with the Treaty of Paris, signed on September 3, 1783. The new 13-state nation's boundaries stretched west to the Mississippi River and included valuable fishing rights around Newfoundland. Eating humble pie, Britain also ceded Florida to Spain.

The Highland Clearances

✦

By 1800 the Scottish highlands had become an overpopulated and uneconomical liability for clan chiefs and other landowners. Their solution was to begin clearing vast tracts of the age-old Caledonian Forest to accommodate flocks of sheep whose meat and wool fetched attractive prices.

Between 1810 and 1820 what became known as the Highland Clearances began in the far northern county of Sutherland. Impossibly high rents were charged crofters who worked the land needed for sheep farms. When these rents could not be met, widescale evictions began – resulting in a mass migration of people from their traditional home-lands.

Some made for the new industrial centers further south, but thousands of others began a mass migration to the newly opened territories of Canada, Australia and New Zealand. A few tried to resist the Clearances with force, winning at least security of tenure and fairer rents. It was too little too late, and by the late 1880s the highlands had become a wilderness populated only by a hardy and stubborn few. And lots of sheep.

Captain Cook:
The Man Who Changed the World

❧

More than any man in history Captain James Cook changed the map of the world and established a number of footholds for British expansion and empire building during the 19th century. A navigator and explorer, Cook also transformed the lot of sailors when he realized that fresh vegetables and fruit extracts could stop them dying from scurvy.

The son of a migrant Scottish farmhand, Cook was born in 1728, in Yorkshire and joined the Royal Navy in 1755. He saw action in the Seven Years' War with France and the navigation charts he made of the St Lawrence River were vital to General Wolfe's amphibious attack on Quebec. Cook explored and mapped the seaways and coasts of Canada in 1759 and 1763 and made the first of three expeditions to the Pacific Ocean in 1768. His commission was to find Terra Australis – a continental landmass believed to exist in the southern seas.

Sailing from Tahiti, Cook "found" and chartered

New Zealand before crossing the Tasman Sea in April 1770 to reach the southern coast of Australia. Presented to King George III on his return to England, Cook was promoted to the rank of commander and set off on two further voyages of discovery and scientific research – in 1772 and 1776. In the course of these he charted Tonga, Easter Island, parts of Antarctica and the south Atlantic island he named South Georgia. His two ships during these trips were the aptly named *Resolution* and *Discovery*.

Cook was killed in 1779, at Kealakekua Bay, Hawaii, during a dispute with native Hawaiians over the theft of a cutter.

The Iron Duke

✦

"**C**ometh the hour, cometh the man" may have been a phrase coined to describe the debt Britain and Europe owed Arthur Wellesley, Duke of Wellington. A military tactician and strategist of genius, it was he whose brilliance helped force the first abdication and exile of Napoleon Bonaparte in 1814, and whose leadership of allied forces at the Battle of Waterloo a year later ended the French emperor's dream of world dominance.

Born in Dublin, the fifth son of the Earl of Mornington, Wellington was educated at Eton College and a French military academy. Commissioned into the army in 1787 – when he was 18 years old – he purchased the rank of lieutenant colonel six years later, saw active service in Flanders and was posted to India in 1796. His success in action resulted in his being knighted when he returned to England in 1805.

After becoming a member of Parliament and spending two years in Ireland as Tory chief secretary,

Wellington returned to action in 1807 – in Copenhagen, where he defeated a small Danish force. It was enough for him to be ordered to Portugal in 1808 when that nation declared war on Napoleon. Victory over French forces at Vimeiro was followed by court-martial for Wellington and senior officers who had prevented him from pursuing the enemy. Acquitted, he returned to Ireland and his former government post, but in 1809 persuaded his political seniors to let him return to Portugal. It was a decision that would prove crucial to Europe.

Capturing Oporto, Wellington saw a joint Anglo-Spanish advance on Madrid fail, despite a victory at Talavera for which he was awarded a peerage. The new viscount retired his army to Portugal. After rein-forcements arrived he was able to capture the Spanish fortresses of Ciudad-Rodrigo and Badajoz in 1812, defeat the French at Salamanca and take Madrid.

In May 1813 Wellington launched a massive offensive against French troops at Vitoria, his victory providing impetus to the European alliance against Napoleon. After further gains at San Sebastien and Pamplona, Wellington marched into France in April 1814 and took Toulouse. The writing clearly on the wall, Napoleon had abdicated four days earlier and was duly exiled to the island of Elba.

Appointed Britain's ambassador to the restored court of Louis XVIII in Paris, Wellington was made a duke and field marshal, granted a sum of £500,000 and a Hampshire estate. He was attending the Congress of Vienna when news reached delegates that Napoleon had escaped from Elba and had formed a new army. Wellington commanded the allied forces (including the army of the Prussian General Gebhard Blücher) which defeated Napoleon at Waterloo, in Belgium, five months later – on June 18.

Weeping as he surveyed the carnage, Wellington is reputed to have said: "I hope to God that I have fought my last battle." He had, but did so with the batons – symbols of a field marshal – of six foreign nations, presented to him in gratitude.

Horatio Nelson

❧

If it was Wellington who masterminded Napoleon's defeat on land, it was Admiral Horatio Nelson who ensured that the French leader was unable to use his navy to expand his empire and ended his plans to invade Britain. And while it was his victory off Cape Trafalgar that effectively annihilated France's maritime force in 1805 – and claimed his life – Nelson's long career included many other triumphs.

The sixth of 11 children of a poor country parson, Nelson was born in 1758. When his mother died, her naval officer brother agreed to take the boy to sea. Nineteen years old when he became a lieutenant, he was promoted to the rank of captain only a year later, when he saw action in the West Indies against a Spanish fleet supporting American revolutionaries.

Married to a young widow, Frances Nisbet, in 1787, Nelson acquired a five-year-old son, Josiah. His career lying fallow for five years (he'd made powerful enemies among British authorities in the West Indies), in January 1793 Nelson was given command of the 64-gun *Agamemnon* and ordered to fight the French in the Mediterranean.

After taking part in successful attempts to capture the Corsican towns of Bastia and Calvi – where his right eye was irreparably damaged by shrapnel – Nelson's success at holding off two Spanish squadrons in the Battle of Cape St Vincent enabled his commander, Sir John Jervis, to gain a major victory. Nelson was rewarded with a knighthood and promotion to the rank of rear admiral. During his next action, at Tenerife in 1797, he lost his left arm.

Armless, but not witless, in 1798 Nelson trapped a French squadron at Alexandria, near the mouth of the Nile and destroyed all 13 of the enemy's ships. Given a hero's welcome in Naples, Nelson embarked on an affair with Emma, wife of the British minister, Sir William Hamilton. Emma would bear him a daughter, Horatia, and Nelson would remain close friends with Sir William – something that would scandalize London society but only enhance Nelson's status with the public.

In 1801 Nelson's success at capturing Copenhagen with a bombardment that left 6,000 Danish defenders dead and wounded raised his stock even higher. When it became clear that Napoleon intended to invade England – with help from the Spanish – in early 1805, Nelson blockaded the port of Toulon. The French squadron there managed to escape to Cadiz and form a combined fleet with Spanish ships. When they emerged on October 20, Nelson and Admiral Cuthbert Collingwood's two divisions were waiting for them.

The Battle of Trafalgar began when Nelson made his famous signal, "England expects that every man will do his duty." They did, and the enemy was torn apart. So, too, was Nelson himself. Fatally wounded by a French sniper's bullet, Nelson died saying: "Now I am satisfied. Thank God, I have done my duty."

That he had. Britain mourned and gave him a state funeral at St Paul's Cathedral. Streets, squares and monuments were named in his honor, and his flagship, *Victory*, was put on permanent display in a Portsmouth dry dock. It was no more than he deserved.

The Abolition of Slavery

❦

For close on 200 years Britain had been a leading player in the world's slave trade, and many a fine family owed its riches to this vile exploitation of their fellow humans. This sad state of affairs finally came to an end in 1807, thanks in large part to the efforts of William Wilberforce.

An evangelical philanthropist, Wilberforce was the son of a wealthy merchant from Hull, Yorkshire. He was educated at Cambridge, where he became friends with the younger William Pitt. Becoming a member of parliament, Wilberforce underwent religious conversion while touring Europe and identified slavery as an evil to be expunged. Working tirelessly with other humanitarians Wilberforce came in for attacks from those with much to lose from abolition.

After winning his fight in Britain, Wilberforce devoted the rest of his life to abolishing the slave trade throughout the world, campaigning for better housing for the poor and being an active member of the London Missionary Society.

George IV

✤

Although the last years of the sad mad George III were a trial for his subjects and ministers, the ten-year reign of his son, George IV, proved even worse. Aged 58 when he finally became king, this George was a wastrel, gambler and self-indulgent fop. He ran up huge personal debts and was an all-round embarrassment.

Married to the probably mad Caroline of Brunswick, George had fallen out with her so absolutely that she was barred from attending his coronation in 1821. Caroline died alone, destitute and broken-hearted. George also married a Catholic widow, Mrs Fitzherbert, in secret. A contravention of the Royal Marriage Act, it had no legal force.

George's patronage of the arts may have resulted in the building of his ornate pavilion at Brighton and London's Regent Street colonnade, but neither was enough to win the affection of a nation more concerned with the often harsh realities of the Industrial Revolution. There was a palpable sigh of relief when George died in 1830, a fat fool mourned only by the sycophantic dandies who filled his court.

Industrial Revolution

❧

By 1800 Britain was the most industrialized country in the world, enjoying an international trade boom, thanks to its own huge natural resources – including coal and iron ore – and a population ready to quit the countryside for work in the factories and mills springing up in small towns that became big cities.

The development of industrial-scale looms and weaving machines, iron and steel works, coal mines and other enterprises offered work for anyone prepared to slave for long hours in brutal conditions where safety was disregarded and environmental pollution was considered an acceptable price to pay for vast profits. Not all employers were uncaring exploiters of workers, some as young as ten years old, but most were.

Raw materials, such as cotton, flowed into British ports from all parts of Britain's fast-growing empire, including the Indian sub-continent, and the newly independent southern United States. The Empire, in turn, proved a captive customer for British products.

Travel and communications would be transformed during the later stages of the Industrial Revolution. A vast network of canals built during the late 18th century would be supplemented by railways which meant that no corner of Britain was too remote, while telegraph lines and wide-circulation newspapers and magazines provided ordinary citizens with information, opinion and news of events far away.

Between 1770 and 1821 the population of Britain rose from about 8.3 million to 14.2 million. A similar population explosion happened in Ireland, which did not have an Industrial Revolution of its own. When that country was struck by famine in the 1840s, the rest of Britain escaped the same fate, even though millions of its citizens now lived in appalling overcrowded tenements and terraces with no sanitation to speak of and work regimes that came close to slavery.

William IV

❧

$\mathfrak{A}$s George IV left no legitimate heirs, Britain's crown went to William, Duke of Clarence – a 60-year-old destined to live only seven years more. Known as "The Sailor King" (he'd served at sea in his youth), William was an honest man, if not over-bright. He was markedly candid in his opinions and refreshingly informal.

The only real crisis of his reign came in 1831 when his prime minister, Lord Grey, suffered the indignity of having his Reform Bill passed by the House of Commons but rejected by the House of Lords. This crucial and long overdue piece of legislation sought to transfer voting privileges from small underpopulated and so-called "rotten" boroughs controlled by nobles and wealthy gentry to heavily populated industrial towns – including Birmingham and Manchester – which were not represented in Parliament at all.

When the Lords rejected two other amended Reform Acts despite a clear national call for their introduction, Grey asked the king to grant him authority to create more than 50 Liberal peers to outvote the Tory majority. William refused and, when Grey threatened to resign, invited the Duke of Wellington to form a new government. The hero of Waterloo was no more successful and William's reluctant agreement in principle to Grey's proposal was threat enough for Tory lords to abstain when the Bill was presented for the last time in June 1832.

Although the Reform Act created 42 new English boroughs, disbanded 56 others and increased the national electorate by 217,000, the working class and many of the lower middle classes remained disenfranchised. It would not be until the Second Reform Act of 1867 (the work of Tory prime minister Benjamin Disraeli) that many working men won the vote, while a third Act (in 1885) extended that right to agricultural workers.

As none of William IV and Queen Adelaide's children survived, Britain's crown passed to the 18-year-old Princess Victoria of Kent – his late brother's daughter – when William died in 1837. A remarkable reign, and age, had begun.

7

The Victorian Age
1837–1901

While history remembers the 64 years of Queen Victoria's reign as the Victorian Age, it was in truth a period dominated by three men – her Prince Consort, Albert, and two outstanding prime ministers, William Gladstone and Benjamin Disraeli. It was they who tutored the queen in affairs of state, steered her through stormy waters and managed a nation which ended the 19th century as the most powerful on earth, with one in four of the world's population a subject of the British Empire.

In the course of her 20-year marriage to Albert, Victoria gave birth to nine children. Her descendants would, in time, succeed to the thrones of Germany, Russia, Denmark, Sweden, Greece, Spain, Yugoslavia and Romania. Her attitudes to foreign affairs were colored by concern for her children's dynasties, especially the German royal families. This led to rows with her ministers on occasions when German interests clashed with Britain's.

Victoria's original mentor, Lord Melbourne, took a back seat when she married her first cousin, Prince Albert of Saxe-Coburg-Gotha, in 1840. It was he who helped shape Victoria's conviction that the monarchy should keep itself clear of transient party politics and take the lead at times of crisis. This philosophy was put into action during the hiatus between 1846 and 1859 when no single party commanded a majority in the House of Commons. It was Victoria who dismissed foreign secretary Lord Palmerston in 1851 and appointed the Lords Rosebery and Aberdeen to high office.

Prince Albert's death from typhoid in 1861 (the Windsor Castle drains were notoriously bad) left Victoria inconsolable. She withdrew from most public appearances for more than a decade, refused to attend the opening of Parliament on seven occasions and devoted her energies to planning and building a series of memorials to her dear departed husband. Public unrest grew with this absentee queen – at least one attempt was made to assassinate her – but it was not until the late 1870s that the charismatic and charming Disraeli coaxed her back. His masterstroke was to declare Victoria Empress of India in 1877.

Although Victoria shared the greatest personal and political rapport with the Conservative leader (he was encouraged to sit and chat with her during official visits), she learned just as much from the Liberal prime minister, Gladstone (who was made to stand throughout their meetings), if only because she was prepared to hear his arguments. They most famously fell out over Gladstone's attempts, during the 1880s and early 1890s, to grant the people of Ireland home rule.

During the last decades of her life Victoria involved herself in state and political matters with remarkable energy and attention to detail. She also, however, denied her wayward son, Edward, access to state papers until 1892. When she died, at her Isle of Wight home, Osborne House, in January 1901, Victoria had reclaimed her nation's trust and love.

The Charge of the Light Brigade

❧

𝔄 disaster that pretty well sums up the chaos and incompetence of the Crimean War, the Charge of the Light Brigade took place near the Russian city of Sebastopol in October 1854. With Russian artillery commanding the heights on each side of a valley at Balaclava, confused signals and the mindless enmity of British commanders Lord Raglan and Lord Cardigan led to an order for the cavalrymen of the Light Brigade to attack Russian positions at the head of that valley. As they tried to do so, almost half of the regiment's 600 men were wiped out.

Turning this military fiasco into a bizarre sort of triumph, Poet Laureate Alfred, Lord Tennyson wrote his jingoistic *Charge of the Light Brigade at Balaclava*. Nothing can disguise the fact that British involvement in this war – between Russia and an alliance of France, Turkey, Austria and Britain dedicated to halting Russian expansion into the Balkans and Scandinavia between 1853 and 1856 – was appallingly planned and executed. The war, however, was won because Russia's military leaders were even worse.

Each side in this conflict lost more than 250,000 men, with atrocious hospital conditions accounting for the disproportionate number of wounded who died of diseases contracted in medical centers. The mythical status of Florence Nightingale – the first woman to run a field hospital and a subsequent lobbyist for improved army conditions – was gained despite the fact that unnecessary fatalities in her hospital exceeded those of the army facilities she so vocally condemned.

The Boer War

✤

If the Crimean War epitomized British military incompetence and arrogance during the 19th century, the Boer War of 1899–1902 represented a remorseless brutal efficiency that reflects little merit on the conduct or characters of British generals Lord Kitchener and Earl Roberts – or Britain's high-handed attitude to any who challenged its supremacy. Kitchener's introduction of what he termed "concentration camps" led directly to the deaths of more than 20,000 women and children.

This conflict was sparked by the refusal of Paul Kruger, president of the Boer (Dutch Afrikaner) South African Republic to grant political rights to the "foreign" – non-Dutch and mostly English – population of Witwatersrand, a province rich in gold mines. His stance was echoed by the Boer leaders of the Orange Free State and Britain launched a major offensive to capture the Transvaal.

The first phase of the war saw Boer victories, most notably in the seiges they laid on the towns of

Mafeking, Ladysmith and Kimberley. Large numbers of British reinforcements arrived from Britain to lift those sieges, but not before the Boers scored a major triumph at Spion Kop, in January 1900. At the height of the Boer War Britain had close to 500,000 troops in South Africa while the Boers numbered no more than 80,000, most of them volunteer farmers.

With Kitchener and Roberts in command, the British began advancing rapidly up the railroad lines. Bloemfontein, Johannesburg and Pretoria were captured during the the first five months of 1900, and while Kruger left the Transvaal for Europe Boer generals Christiaan de Wet and Jacobus De la Rey kept large rural areas of the Transvaal and the Orange Free State from falling into British hands.

Pursuing a scorched earth policy, Kitchener began destroying Boer farms and rounding up civilians for his death camps. Although General Jan Smuts would lead his forces to within 50 miles of the British garrison of Cape Town in late 1900, the Boers could not hope to prevail. In May 1902 they finally accepted the loss of their independence and Britain won unhindered access to South Africa's vast gold reserves.

The Irish Potato Famine

❦

One of the greatest natural disasters to strike the Western world in modern times, the potato famine that hit Ireland between 1845 and 1850 resulted in more than one million deaths and the enforced emigration of a million more. Its effects would not have been a tenth as bad if the British government of the time had made the slightest effort to relieve the starvation, and if mostly absentee landlords had not made matters worse by evicting countless thousands of stricken tenants from land made barren by successive crop failures.

Although the potato blight brought widespread suffering throughout Europe, Ireland suffered worse because of the population's almost complete reliance on the potato as a staple diet. Ireland's corn crops – which remained unaffected – could have saved the day had they been made available to the Irish poor, but harvests continued to be exported. Profit, it seems, counted more than human lives.

Understandable outrage at Britain's apparent lack

of concern inevitably led to growing calls for Irish independence and the creation of ever more powerful political coalitions. But it would be 70 long years before Ireland would be granted its wish and a new Republic would be born.

Charles Dickens: The Great Storyteller

❖

Arguably the greatest English novelist of all time, Charles Dickens married a fine sense of the absurd with a keen eye for detail, an awareness of social issues that "polite" Victorian society preferred to ignore, and a talent that rarely let him down. His overwhelming popularity with queen and commoners alike was greatly helped by the serialization of some of his best works in monthly magazines. These achieved huge sales and made best-sellers of such works as *The Pickwick Papers*, *Oliver Twist*, *Nicholas Nickleby*, *Barnaby Rudge* and *The Old Curiosity Shop*. The death of Little Nell, heroine of the last-named book, resulted in a national mourning as profound as any given a real-life person.

Born in Portsmouth, Hampshire, in 1812, Dickens began his working life only 12 years later, when his father – a navy office pay clerk – was declared bankrupt and imprisoned. Set to manual work in a London blacking factory, the young boy would draw on those early experiences to create the often painful pictures of working-class life that so stirred social consciences in later years.

After finding work as a reporter in the House of Commons, Dickens's breakthrough came with the appearance of his first episodes of *The Pickwick Papers* in 1836. Eventually a very rich man, Dickens used his wealth and preeminence to campaign for the causes closest to his heart – including the anti-slavery movement, social housing projects and inter-national copyright laws. He also traveled extensively in Europe and the United States, where his reading "concerts" were the hottest tickets of the day.

He died in 1870 leaving a mass of timeless tales for future generations to enjoy and gain a glimpse of what it really meant to live in the Victorian Age.

8

The Twentieth Century

❖

The Playboy King

❖

The second child and eldest son of Victoria and Albert, Edward VII was 60 years old when he finally ascended to the throne in 1901. So dismissive was his mother towards him that Edward had even been excluded from seeing official state documents until he reached the age of 50. Apart from creating him Prince of Wales (merely in keeping with tradition) Victoria had not given him any public role worth mentioning.

An affable and popular man, Edward would prove an able monarch, his easy sophistication charming all who met him. Educated at Oxford and Cambridge

Universities, he established his waywardness in 1861 by dallying with an actress while serving with an army unit in Ireland. That first of many scandals coincided with the rapid decline and death of his father and Victoria could never separate the two events in her mind. Although he was married two years later to the handsome Alexandra, a Danish princess, Edward continued to enjoy a sporting life – he was a keen racegoer, yachtsman and game hunter – and the company of beautiful women. One of his mistresses was the celebrated actress, Lilly Langtry.

A competent French speaker (he enjoyed numerous sojourns in Parisian bordellos), Edward's use of that language during a state visit to Paris resulted in a wave of popularity there, a thawing of relations between long-frosty neighbors, and the creation of the 1904 Anglo-French Entente Cordiale.

Relations with his nephew Wilhelm II, emperor of Germany, were not so easy. Edward was concerned by and suspicious of the Kaiser's build-up of military and naval resources, and supported the reforms initiated by his own Secretary of State for War, Richard Bourdon, and the First Sea Lord, Sir John Fisher. Edward's death in 1910 meant he did not live to see his suspicions about Wilhelm confirmed. But his support for Bourdon and Fisher meant that Britain was much better prepared when World War I started four years later.

George V

❦

Having suffered the exclusion imposed by his mother, Edward VII made certain that his son George did not come to the throne unprepared. Becoming his father's heir in 1892 when his older brother, Prince Albert, died, George ended his naval career and began the training his father initiated and encouraged. He would need it.

George V was confronted by many crises during his 26-year reign, including World War I, Ireland's fight for – and winning of – independence, women's battle to secure the vote, the General Strike of the 1920s, the Great Depression of the 1930s and the rise of Hitler's Nazis. And while the government of Britain and its empire rested ever more in the hands of elected politicians, the king proved a wise counsel for successive prime ministers. He could also exercise his authority when necessary and it was his selection of the Conservative Party's Stanley Baldwin as prime minister in 1923 which helped bring a satisfactory end to the power vacuum caused by the resignation of

Andrew Bonar Law.

Although he was in poor health for the last eight years of his life, George was able to enjoy the celebrations to mark his silver jubilee in 1935 and witness the real affection in which he was held.

World War I

❧

This was a conflict that was bound to happen sooner or later. By the day in June 1914 that a Serbian nationalist assassinated the Austrian Archduke Ferdinand in Sarajevo, Germany, Austria-Hungary and Turkey had formed an alliance clearly intent on attacking France to the west and Russia to the east. Both nations had territories the Germans believed to be theirs, though these were only a justification for a policy of general expansion by all three members of what was known as the Central Powers. Aware of this – and a frightening build-up of German armaments – Britain, France, Russsia, Italy and Japan had united in their own alliance and were determined to meet and defeat any aggression.

Ferdinand's death gave the Central Powers their excuse to mobilize and when Germany outflanked France's main defensive forces to sweep across Belgium, Britain was obliged to declare war on August 4. A British Expeditionary Force united with the French army to halt the German advance on

Paris. As both sides dug in, they little knew that it would be four long years before the Great War shuddered to a halt.

During those four years British troops also saw action in the Dardanelles and Gallipoli where – despite the valiant support of Australian and New Zealand troops – they failed to invade Turkey. In Mesopotamia and Egypt they were aided by the Arab forces marshaled by T.E. Lawrence – "Lawrence of Arabia." Russia's early success in advancing into East Prussia, German Poland and Galicia was overturned by a massive German offensive in 1915. Widespread discontent at Russian generals' handling of the war would help fuel the political unrest that climaxed in the Russian Revolution of 1917.

It was the unrelenting slaughter of the Western Front – and the lack of any real progress – that turned British public opinion from the patriotic fervor exhibited by astonishing recruitment figures in the first months of the war (when the promise was that it would be "over by Christmas") to open criticism of the five-man War Cabinet led by Liberal prime minister David Lloyd George, none of whose war policies seemed any better than those of his predecessor and fellow Liberal, Lord Asquith.

In truth, the Western Front stalemate was due entirely to appalling military leadership. Kaiser Wilhelm characterized this by describing British troops as "lions led by donkeys." When Field Marshal Douglas Haig was told that 60,000 of his men had been killed or seriously wounded in the first day of the Battle of the Somme – July 1, 1916 – he simply ordered the continuation of a massacre that would continue for five months and result in no real territorial gains. The German command, it must be said, was no better.

The United States, meanwhile, maintained a strict observance of its neutrality in foreign wars, even shipping supplies to both sides of the war at first. Germany's introduction of its secret weapon – the submarine – and its stupidity in sinking US ships that sailed into embargoed waters, forced President Woodrow Wilson to declare war against Germany in 1917. By September 1918, no fewer than 1,2000,000 US troops were "over there." Their presence tipped the military balance and the Allied advance began.

By mid-October 1918 almost all of German-occupied France and part of Belgium had been taken. Civilian and military unrest mounted in Germany and on November 9 the Kaiser abdicated. Two days later, in the French town of Redonthes, the Armistice was signed to bring World War I to an end. Described as "the war to end all wars," it would sadly prove nothing of the sort.

Independence for Ireland

❧

Even as World War I captured most of David Lloyd George's attention when he became head of the War Cabinet in December 1916, Britain was struggling to maintain control of Ireland, where calls for Home Rule had changed to full-blown demands for independence.

Matters had come to a head in Easter that year when members of the Irish Republican Brotherhood led by Patrick Pearse and Tom Clarke, along with the Irish Citizen Army – an association of Dublin workers founded after a failed general strike in 1913 – and the small Sinn Féin Party, combined to stage an armed nationwide insurrection.

In the event, the Easter Rebellion would be confined to Dublin. On April 21 British intelligence officers had captured the Irish nationalist Sir Roger Casement in County Kerry and charged him with smuggling arms from Germany. Alarmed, the leader of the Irish Volunteers, Eoin MacNeill, canceled orders for the mobilization of his rebels. Pearse and

Clarke went ahead with their plans, however, and on Easter Monday some 1,560 Irish Volunteers and 200 Irish Citizen Army members were involved in actions which saw Dublin's Post Office and other strategic points captured, and Pearse's reading of a proclamation declaring the birth of an Irish republic.

Britain's response was rapid and brutally effective. Troops poured into Dublin and artillery bombardments shattered the city center. Pearse and 14 other leaders of the rebellion were seized, court-martialed and executed. Revulsion at this made martyrs out of men whose support had not been universal. The Anglo-Irish government collapsed and Britain was unable – despite imposing a repressive military regime – to resist the inexorable rise of a nationalist movement that would claim victory when the Irish Free State was created on December 6, 1921.

Votes for Women!

❧

The British government's decision to grant women the vote in May 1928 was a victory for common sense – and for Emmeline Pankhurst, the woman who'd waged a 40-year "war" to win political equality for half the population. There were others who carried the suffrage banner high, but it was Mrs Pankhurst – and her daughter Christabel – who became preeminent in that struggle.

Born Emmeline Goulden in 1858, in 1879 she married lawyer Richard Pankhurst, author of the first female suffrage bill in the late 1860s and of two Married Women's Property Acts during the following decades. Holding a number of municipal offices in her native Manchester, she increasingly devoted her time and energies to the Women's Social and Political Union (WSPU), which she founded in 1903. This first attracted national attention two years later when Christabel and Annie Kenney were ejected from a Liberal Party meeting in Manchester, arrested for a technical assault on police outside, and imprisoned when they refused to pay fines.

From 1906 Emmeline directed WSPU affairs from London, campaigning against Liberal candidates at elections and ending up in prison three times between 1908 and 1909. From July 1912 the WSPU became more militant. Christabel directed an arson campaign from Paris while other members instigated a disruptive publicity offensive which saw hundreds of them incarcerated. Force feeding was introduced when they staged hunger strikes and only the outbreak of World War I forced Emmeline to suspend militant action.

Moving to the United States, Emmeline visited Canada and Russia to promote the industrial mobilization of women. She lived in the US, Canada and Bermuda at the war's end, but in 1926 returned to England to stand as a Conservative candidate in a London constituency. Her health failed before she could be elected, but she lived long enough to see the passing of the Representation of the People Act vindicate her long battle.

The General Strike

❧

David Lloyd George had promised everyone who limped back from World War I that Britain would be "a land fit for heroes." Within four years he would be ousted from power and the premiership won by the Conservative Party's Andrew Bonar Law. He managed to hold power for only five months, his management of negotiating the terms of Britain's war debt to the United States – which were not as favorable as Britain had expected – forcing his resignation in May 1923. Nine months later his successor, Stanley Baldwin, had resigned too, when his demand for a mandate to reverse Bonar Law's free-trade policy was rejected by Parliament.

The land fit for heroes was becoming a mismanaged shambles. No one was in power long enough to address the real problems of industrial unrest caused by rampant inflation, breadline wages and a slump in the coal trade. It came as no surprise that the Labour Party won enough seats in the ensuing election for Ramsay MacDonald to become Britain's first socialist prime minister.

During his 11-month tenure, MacDonald recognized the Soviet regime in Russia and averted violence in Ireland by canceling the Irish Free State's debt to Britain in return for it abandoning all claims to the six northern counties of Ulster. Problems still plagued Britain and the return of Baldwin in November 1924 signaled an economic policy guaranteed to make the situation worse. A 40 per cent income tax and a 50 per cent excess profits tax only made life tougher for those at the bottom and gave those at the top every excuse to keep wages pegged at a minimal level.

A further slump in the coal trade during 1925 gave Britain's miners no alternative but to call a nationwide strike. Other workforces announced their support and on May 4, 1926 the General Strike began. Baldwin declared a state of emergency, persuaded volunteers to maintain essential services and refused to negotiate with labor leaders until the strike was called off. Although the miners would continue their struggle for some months more, all other workers returned to work only eight days later. No storm in a teacup, the General Strike gave notice to the British establishment that the workers had muscles they were prepared to flex, and they could bring the nation to a halt if they wanted.

Love Conquers All

❧

The death of George V, and the succession of his son Edward in January 1936, pitched Britain into the gravest constitutional crisis of modern times. A lively, likeable and sociable man, the 40-year-old Prince of Wales was deeply and openly in love with Mrs Wallis Simpson, an American divorcee whom he could not marry (Britain's sovereigns are constitutionally head of an Anglican Church which does not sanction the remarriage of divorced persons) and would not abandon.

After months of discussion and negotiation, Edward VIII chose love over duty and announced his abdication before being crowned. In December his brother, Albert, Duke of York, was declared (confusingly) King George VI. One of his first acts was to create Edward the Duke of Windsor. Edward and Mrs Simpson went into a voluntary exile for life, spending most of their last years together in Paris. They now lie together in a royal family tomb at Frogmore, near Windsor.

George VI

❧

Completely unprepared for the duties of kingship, George VI's successful negotiation of the stormy waters which faced him during his 16-year reign are testament both to his character and the support he had from his queen – the redoubtable Elizabeth Bowes-Lyon, youngest daughter of the 14th Earl of Strathmore and Kinghorne – whom he'd married in 1923, three years after he'd been created Duke of York.

In 1921 he sponsored an annual camp, at which equal numbers of public school and working-class youths spent a week together as his guests – a far-sighted piece of social engineering typical of a man who chose to remain in London with his beleaguered subjects throughout World War II when his ministers wanted the royal family in safer quarters.

Before that war began in 1939, George consolidated Anglo-French solidarity and formed a close friendship with US President Franklin D. Roosevelt. Like many in the British establishment he supported prime minister Neville Chamberlain's policy of appeasement with the bellicose Adolf Hitler. When Chamberlain was forced to resign in 1940, he unreservedly supported Winston Churchill.

In the years following World War II George had the difficult task of ruling an empire that began to shrink when India and Pakistan won their independence and a new, more egalitarian Commonwealth of Nations was created. At home the overwhelming victory of a socialist Labour government and the birth of a welfare state were challenges he tackled by observing the limitations of a constitutional monarchy. He brought throne and people closer by being the first ruler to broadcast on radio – an achievement all the greater for his having to overcome the handicap of a severe stammer.

Suffering poor health from 1948, George VI died in 1952 – a few months after undergoing surgery for lung cancer.

World War II

❧

The only truly global war in history, World War II was actually a number of separate conflicts which began for different reasons, overlapped and ended together in 1945. Its genesis was the election of Adolf Hitler as chancellor of Germany in 1933 – a man set on reversing Germany's defeat in World War I and establishing a Nazi empire over Europe. In September 1939 he invaded Poland after signing a non-aggression pact with the Soviet leader, Josef Stalin. Two days later Britain and France – who'd given Poland security guarantees – declared war on Germany. They did not, however, declare war on the Soviet Union when it too invaded Poland.

Hitler moved quickly, advancing after the deceptive quiet of winter (a period known as "the phony war") to occupy Denmark and Norway in May 1940. On May 10 a discredited Chamberlain resigned in London, Winston Churchill was appointed to head a wartime coalition government and Hitler launched an offensive that would see Holland and Belgium in

German hands within weeks. Anglo-French forces in Belgium were beaten back to the French coast at Dunkirk, where 338,000 men were miraculously evacuated. Shortly after, the Germans took Paris and Italy declared war on France and Britain.

Amazingly, Britain's relatively small air defenses managed to inflict enough damage on the German Luftwaffe through the following months (a conflict known as "The Battle of Britain") for Hitler to shelve his plans for a full-scale invasion. During the next two years British cities – most especially London – were subjected to intensive bombing ("the Blitz") that had less to do with strategic targets than massacring helpless civilians.

Churchill feared that Britain would survive only if the United States joined the war, but President Franklin D. Roosevelt was forced by public opinion to restrict US involvement to supplying Britain with weapons. Italian forces in North Africa were routed by General Wavell late in 1940, but in early 1941 Italian and German troops attacked Yugoslavia, Greece and the island of Crete while German Field Marshal Erwin Rommel led an Axis return to North Africa.

Britain's chief naval campaign for the next two

years was in the North Atlantic against packs of German submarines intent on eliminating US supplies and British troop movements. Thanks to a fantastic surge in munitions production and a number of scientific advances, Britain began to cancel Germany's initial advantage. Hitler aided that by foolishly attacking his supposed ally, Russia, in June 1941. The massive force he diverted to the Eastern Front would be bogged down and eventually beaten by a Soviet resistance that lost a staggering 20 million casualties in the process. Stalin signed a mutual assistance treaty with Britain to stack the odds against Hitler.

On the far side of the globe Japan was already waging war against China, but on December 7, 1941 attacked the US Pacific Fleet at Pearl Harbor, Hawaii as a preliminary to seizing British, French and Dutch colonies in South-East Asia. When America and Britain declared war on Japan the next day, a truly worldwide war began.

Although the German-Italian-Japanese Axis was at its strongest in early 1942 – the Japanese captured Singapore from Britain in February to begin the decline of British power in Asia, while German forces laying siege to Leningrad were reinforced by troops attacking Stalingrad. With most of eastern Europe under his control Hitler began to implement his "final solution," the extermination of six million Jews, gypsies and others in concentration camps.

Churchill, Roosevelt and Stalin agreed a policy of beating Germany before Japan. The defeat of Rommel in North Africa by the British Eighth Army of General Montgomery (the last UK force to fight without US troops) marked the turning point in Hitler's western front. In July 1943 British and US forces invaded Sicily and, two months later, the Italian mainland. Italy surrendered and switched sides, but it would not be until June 1944 that a stubborn German defense was overcome and Rome could be liberated. On the eastern front Germany suffered defeat at Kursk, the biggest tank battle in history, and in January 1944 the siege of Leningrad – the longest in modern history – was lifted by the Soviet army. Hitler was on the retreat, his homeland now subjected to massive continuous air raids by Allied bombers.

On June 6, 1944 the Allies launched their long-awaited attack on Germany's forces in Normandy, western France. Paris was liberated on August 25 after bitter fighting across France, followed quickly by the rest of France and Belgium.

Germany launched its final defensive assault through the Ardennes region of Belgium ("the Battle of the Bulge") in December 1944, but was beaten back. The Allies crossed the Rhine in March 1945 while Soviet troops fought their way to Berlin from the east. They reached the German capital first, in April, and linked with US troops shortly after. On April 30 Adolf Hitler committed suicide in his bombproof shelter while the rest of Berlin stood in ruins. German forces surrendered in Italy on May 2 and in Germany itself five days later.

The war with Japan now reached its terrible conclusion. British forces under General Slim – with help from the guerrilla-fighting Chindits led by Orde Wingate – had evicted the Japanese from Burma, their last Asian mainland stronghold, in July 1944. Japan now held many Pacific islands, and it would take many months of brutal fighting for US amphibious forces to capture them one by one. Casualties on both sides were horrific – most especially at Okinawa, which saw more US marines land on its beaches than the entire Allied force that came ashore in Normandy.

With their mainland subjected to bombing raids and a naval blockade, Japan's generals refused to surrender. The dropping of atomic bombs on Hiroshima and Nagasaki on August 6 and 9 – together with a belated Soviet declaration of war and invasion of Japanese-ruled Manchuria on August 8 – forced Japan's unconditional surrender on August 14. World War II was finally over.

Sir Winston Churchill

❦

A charismatic personality, gifted orator and a renaissance man who wrote extensively and painted pleasingly, Winston Churchill was also an obstinate and sometimes feckless man capable of making enemies of life-long friends and – disastrously for a politician – often incapable of following a party line. Not the kind you'd expect to prove a leader of genius when your country is facing its greatest peril. But he was.

Grandson of the 7th Duke of Marlborough and son of Lord Randolph Churchill and his American wife, Jennie Jerome, the young Winston was educated at Harrow School and served in the army before becoming a war correspondent in the Boer War. He entered Parliament as a Conservative in 1900 but defected to the Liberals four years later. He was Home Secretary under Lord Asquith and became First Lord of the Admiralty in 1911.

Four years later he resigned in protest at Britain's failure in the Dardanelles campaign, rejoined the army as a battalion commander, but was invited to serve in Lloyd George's post-World War I coalition, first as minister of munitions, then as secretary for air and war, finally as colonial secretary. Losing his seat in 1922, he spent two years writing a five-volume history of World War I before returning to Parliament – as a Conservative once more.

As Chancellor of the Exchequer between 1924 and 1929 he returned Britain to the Gold Standard and took a hard line during the General Strike. The fall of Baldwin's government in 1929 saw Churchill cast into something of a political wilderness during the 1930s. He was not the first to balk at Britain's attempts to appease Hitler, but became one of Chamberlain's most vocal opponents. Germany's invasion of Poland in 1939 vindicated Churchill's stance. After a spell as first lord of the Admiralty he was an obvious first choice to head the wartime coalition.

Defeat in the general election of 1945 embittered Churchill greatly, but he concentrated his efforts at promoting his belief that Soviet domination of eastern Europe posed a real threat to the world as a whole. In 1946, during a speech in Fulton, Missouri, he coined the phrase "Iron Curtain" to dramatize Soviet intransigence. Returned as prime minister in

1951, Churchill's last years in office were plagued by illness. He was 80 years old when, in 1955, he passed the Conservative leadership to Anthony Eden.

Down, but not out, he published his four-volume *History of the English-Speaking Peoples* in 1956-58. Deciding not to stand for reelection in the 1964 election, Churchill died, aged 90, a few months later. Fittingly, he was accorded a state funeral – the first commoner to be given that honor since the Duke of Wellington in 1852.

A Social Revolution

❖

Although Britain was grateful to Winston Churchill for the job he'd done during the war, his Conservative Party was not forgiven for its many shortcomings before it. In the general election called in late 1945, the Labour Party of Clement Attlee (who'd served as Churchill's deputy in the wartime coalition) swept to power with a massive majority.

It did so promising the greatest social revolution in British history: the coal and railway industries were to be nationalized and a comprehensive welfare state created. Health and hospital care were to be free for all, and a national insurance scheme introduced to ensure that everyone received a state pension on retirement.

During his six years in power, Attlee granted India its independence as quickly as he could, aligned Britain with the US as the Cold War with the Soviet Union and Communist China escalated, helped found NATO, provided massive support for the Berlin airlift when Russia seized half of Germany, and was the first US ally to contribute troops to the Korean War when Chinese-backed North Korea attempted to take the whole country.

Attlee could also be high-handed and the Labour Party was split when it learned that he'd secretly authorized the construction of a British atomic bomb. Although Labour was returned to power in the election of 1950, its majority was cut to ten. Key cabinet members resigned in protest at the cost of the Korean War and the imposition of charges for some health services. Forced to call a new election, Attlee and the Labour Party were beaten and a Conservative government led by Winston Churchill took over. Four years later Attlee retired, handing the reins of Labour Party leadership to Hugh Gaitskell.

Elizabeth II:
A Truly Modern Monarch

❖

Britain's present queen was on holiday in Kenya with her husband Philip, Duke of Edinburgh, when she received word that her father had died. It was 1952 and she was 26 years old – a woman raised with a keen sense of responsibility and encouraged, from an early age, to use the modern technologies of newsreel film and radio as a marketing tool. Her coronation, in 1953, was the first to be televised and understandably attracted an audience of millions around the world.

Elizabeth's reign has seen ten prime ministers come and go – Sir Winston Churchill, Sir Anthony Eden, Harold Macmillan, Sir Alec Douglas-Home (all Conservatives), Harold Wilson and James Callaghan (Labour), Edward Heath, Margaret Thatcher, John Major (Conservative), and the present occupant of 10 Downing Street, Labour leader Tony Blair. It is widely accepted that the queen's years of experience make her an able counsellor for those of her ministers prepared to consult her in difficult times – of which there have been many.

British forces have seen action in many theaters of war since 1952, including the armed struggles for independence in former colonies Cyprus and Kenya, the British retaliation when Egyptian leader Colonel Abdul Gamal Nasser seized control of the Suez Canal in 1956, and the 1982 Falklands Campaign of Margaret Thatcher to regain control of the South Atlantic archipelago claimed by Argentina. Most damagingly, British troops have been based in Ulster for the best part of 30 years, attempting to police a state of civil war between intransigent extremists from the nationalist community seeking union with the Republic of Ireland and loyalists wishing to preserve Northern Ireland's constitutional links with the rest of Britain.

Britain's military capabilities are currently mostly dedicated to helping form "peace-keeping" forces under the aegis of the United Nations or NATO – most notably as part of the multinational force that took part in the Desert Storm offensive that drove Iraqi troops out of Kuwait in 1991, and the most recent conflict in the former Yugoslavia.

During Elizabeth's reign Britain became a member

of the European Union and has now decided to give the people of Scotland and Wales their own legislative assemblies – a move which could conceivably lead to either seeking full-blown independence, so making her United Kingdom a thing of the past.

On a more personal note, the queen has been proven no less prone to the modern ailments of divorce and separation. Three of her children – Charles, the Prince of Wales, Anne, the Princess Royal, and Andrew, the Duke of York – have seen their marriages founder, along with that of her younger sister, Princess Margaret, Countess Snowdon. The tragic death of Princess Diana in 1998 pitched Britain into a storm of recrimination that forced the royal family to reevaluate its public image and future role, which it appears to be doing with some success.

As the world faces the uncertainties of a new millennium, Britain too is having to find a role in which its undoubted qualities can be best employed, its history and past experience its greatest asset on a globe still riven by dissent, rivalry and aggression as new and younger nations try to establish their own claims on the future.